UNMASKING

The Coach's Guide to Impostor Syndrome

TARA HALLIDAY

R∃THINK PRESS

First published in Great Britain 2018
by Rethink Press (www.rethinkpress.com)

© Copyright Tara Halliday

Cover image © Ryan Cowan Photography

Praise

'Tara Halliday has written an invaluable reference for coaches on impostor syndrome; it is both insightful and instructive. What really resonated for me was her own openness and candour, and the clarity that she brings to understanding this topic.

I coach a lot of successful leaders, and too many feel undeserving of the praise and accolades they receive, and privately self-report feelings of inadequacy and even fraudulence. I found this book thought provoking, yes, but importantly a handy resource containing well-conceived and practical coaching strategies.

Tara brings both rigour and commercial smarts to this topic, underpinned by a genuine concern for helping clients alleviate the discomfort and distress they experience, which can rob them needlessly of authentic feelings of success. Recommended reading.'

Andrew Priestley, business leadership coach,
The Coaching Experience (global consultancy)

'*Unmasking* is an excellent, very thorough, deep-dive into the little-known phenomenon of impostor syndrome. Tara has unpacked and explained what is really going on when a successful high-achiever feels like an impostor.

I've not seen any other book that explains this topic so well and provides coaches with a clear method for helping clients to achieve their full potential and feel fully worthy of their success. If you want your clients to enjoy life at the top, get this book.'

Ben Green, executive coach and author of *Lead with Confidence – A Guide for Newly Promoted Senior Managers*

'Tara's book was such an eye-opener for me. Her ability to demystify and deconstruct a very complex and often misunderstood phenomenon that affects 70% of high achievers is a true gift.

This book will undoubtedly help many others who may be suffering in silence or even contemplating quitting! I, for one, am so grateful to her for writing it.'

Susan Payton, story strategist, The Business of Stories, co-author of *Fit for Purpose Leadership #1*

'What I loved about this book was that as I read it, I started to notice some of these behaviours in my clients and friends. Suddenly things that should already have been obvious to me were staring me in the face. With the wonderful advice offered I was able to respond more effectively. Not only that, I saw some of me in her words, which made me smile. Personal growth is never-ending and I believe that the right message will reach you when you need to hear it. My hope is that this book will support other coaches in the way that it has me.'

Dale Darley, coach, writer and author, Soul Writers Academy

Contents

Introduction

I have a PhD in engineering as a result of impostor syndrome. I had no idea at the time, but now it's clear.

This is typical of a phenomenon that affects 70% of high achievers.[1] Impostor syndrome is the secret feeling of being a fraud and the fear of being found out. The secrecy means that few people talk about it and so it often goes unrecognised. It creates confusion, anxiety and stress-related illness, and can lead to people ending their careers. In my case, it led to me getting a PhD.

Impostor syndrome is not a psychological disorder requiring psychiatric care. Strictly speaking it is a 'phenomenon'; a recognised pattern of emotional stress and destructive behaviours that sabotages well-being. *Unmasking* is for coaches aiming to help their clients overcome this debilitating problem.

I have used several case studies in this book, including my own experiences, to illustrate what you may come across in your coaching. For confidentiality, I have changed minor details and names. Any similarity between these case studies and people you know are coincidental, but will go to show how common such experiences are.

My impostor syndrome

When starting my research, I recognised my own impostor behavioural traits: perfectionism, approval-seeking, intolerance of my mistakes, and needing to be right. However, feeling like a fraud did not resonate with me. When a journalist asked me about impostor syndrome, I even replied, 'No, I haven't experienced it myself.' As my research continued, though, I realised that I avoided leadership roles. Avoiding specific activities or challenges is typical behaviour for someone with impostor syndrome, so I did have it after all.

When I was growing up, my only model of leadership was of the directive kind. I must emphasise it was not my family's fault at all: they had never learned a better model of leadership, either. My first experience of failing at leadership was being promoted to patrol leader in the Girl Guides at the age of fourteen. As a naturally caring person, I liked people to be happy, so the directive leadership style I'd learned didn't work for me. However, I didn't see this as a lack of leadership skills, or a need to find a leadership style more suited to my personality. Instead, I was uncomfortable and felt like a horrible person.

At the age of sixteen, I won a scholarship to a college dedicated to bringing together future leaders and promoting international peace and understanding. As is typical for someone with impostor syndrome, I made excuses for the fact I'd won the scholarship: the selectors had a comparatively small group to choose from; they felt sorry for my low-income background; they chose me due to positive action. I didn't believe I had earned my scholarship fairly, so I felt I didn't belong at the college. Conveniently, I took this to mean the school's hope that the students would go on to become leaders did not apply to me.

After university, I applied for a job with a global engineering company. My psychometric test revealed an unusual psychological profile typical of top management. The recruiter was excited and offered me a fast-track to a management position – which I turned down. I told myself it sounded boring.

At the time, a friend was starting a PhD programme, and I decided, 'If he can do that, so can I.' Studying was a comfortable area for me. All the while, I had no idea I was running away from a fear of failing at being a leader.

It could be because of perfectionism that I never felt my leadership style was good enough. I focused on my errors, not my successes. Years later, when a leaving employee told me I was the best boss he'd ever had, I was stunned, but I quickly dismissed his comment as an anomaly. My issue was not just my leadership skill, but also the stress the role caused me and the feeling of not being good enough. That included feeling like I was an unpopular and ineffective leader.

I interpreted my (perceived) poor leadership as a personality flaw, not as an area in which I could have improved. At the time, I reported to the company CEO, who was a superb leader. I was amazed at how brilliantly he motivated people, but I put it down to him being a better person than me, a nice guy. It didn't occur to me to ask him for help or mentoring, which I know he would have been delighted to give. And he had no idea how much I was struggling.

My stress continued to increase and I became argumentative in meetings. Afterwards, I would feel ashamed of my behaviour, which felt a little out of my control. It made me dislike myself and ask, 'What's wrong with me?' Eventually, I left not only the job, but the whole field due to a convenient back injury.

In running from leadership, I chose a career as a holistic (whole person) therapist and transformational coach. Other part-time work included being a lettings agent, estate agent, call-centre debt collector, and one summer in a garden centre. Nothing successful or glamorous, and my salary was one-tenth of what it had been in my previous career. The impostor behaviours came up from time to time, but to a lesser degree. It was manageable.

In 2013 I started a property investor accelerator programme. Unfortunately for me, there was competition, learning and lots of praise for succeeding. It was an exciting programme, but it provoked my innate impostor behaviours.

Mid-programme, I was flying high and set to gain top results. Then, as is common in property, two of my big deals fell through. Suddenly, I was looking at no longer being the best. I was also in a difficult home environment, and didn't have the emotional support I'd had in my engineering career; I fell hard and fast. Getting out of bed was hard. For a high-energy, capable person that was a frightening place to find myself in. Suicide even sounded like a sensible option compared to the shame of what I saw as failure. Despite many years of supporting others through trying times, I could not pull myself together.

Luckily for me, I found some help. A friend who was going through a messy divorce was happier and more peaceful each time we met. And I was getting unhappier each time we met. Desperate for a solution, I jumped into the programme that was working for him – deep transformational work creating unconditional worth. Within days, I was feeling brighter, and within a few months, I was happier than I had ever been in my life.

And it continued to improve, even though none of my outer circumstances had changed. Indeed, the following year I went through even greater financial challenges, but this time I faced them calmly, without upset or drama. I was delighted, because I had made a lasting change in my life.

What this book offers

In 1978, Clance and Imes[2] described the new phenomenon of impostor behaviour, and it has since become more widely recognised. Certain myths have also arisen: that it is a lack of confidence, low self-esteem or incompetence. None of these is true, and as a coach, you need to know how best to help your client. Impostor syndrome will come up whether you're a life coach, business coach, team leader, mentor, counsellor or priest.

Armed with this guide, you will be able to identify impostor feelings and behaviours and relieve the confusion they cause. You will discover the root cause of impostor syndrome and what exacerbates it, and help your clients overcome it in practical, proven ways. If, like I was, the sufferer is unaware of impostor syndrome, then they may believe their issues relate to personality, executive stress or work–life balance, to name a few. As a coach, you are better placed than most to hear your clients' secret fears.

As a bonus, the secret to overcoming impostor syndrome is also the secret to achieving peak performance and reaching maximum human potential. This means that your work will take people from being stressed to achieving greater results than they would ever have thought possible.

Typical impostor sufferers do not tell their family, friends or colleagues about their fear of being found out as a fraud. However, they are likely to reveal their secret feelings to a neutral, confidential party. Coaches are ideally positioned to hear and help. By coach, I also mean business leaders coaching their team, mentors, counsellors, advisors and priests. I say 'coach' for simplicity. If you coach high-achievers, whether they acknowledge their success or not, then you will eventually come across impostor syndrome.

How to use this book

Unmasking is divided into three sections. Part 1 describes what impostor syndrome is – the symptoms; the effect on sufferers; the myths; situations that trigger and intensify it. In Part 2, we delve into the underlying cause of impostor syndrome, why it develops and its impact on people's lives. We also explore the solution to eradicating it and the principles coaches can use daily.

Part 3 is guidance for people coaching impostor sufferers – how to help, what to avoid, and attitude. It explains the process for working through the emotional issues without becoming stuck in an endless loop. We discuss managing the trigger situations proactively so that your clients don't fall prey to it again.

Coaches tend to have good self-awareness. I encourage you to draw on your personal experiences as you work through this book, because they will be valuable in helping others.

I have designed this book to be useful to all four Honey and Mumford learning types:[3] reflector, theorist, pragmatist and activist. For reflectors, who like to observe and consider things, Part 1 demonstrates what impostor syndrome looks like and its effects. Theorists will enjoy the 'Why' in Part 2, to get to the heart of the issue. Pragmatists will find practical step-by-step guides to identifying impostor patterns and working with clients throughout the book. If you're an activist, you'll be most interested in Part 3. See for yourself how it all works, but do read all parts of the book to gain the deep understanding that will make your coaching more powerful.

Since 2001, I have been a therapist and transformational coach helping people through personal difficulties, reducing stress and becoming calmer and happier. This work is a delight and privilege. My passion for helping people feel better is described beautifully in the prayer 'May all living beings be free from suffering'.

Suffering here does not mean the everyday pain of life, like breaking a toe or having your car stolen. It refers to emotional distress based on the meaning people give to negative events, and impostor syndrome is one form of emotional distress. My dearest wish is that you will apply my practical tools for reducing impostor syndrome in your work. Together, we can reach more people and relieve more suffering.

1. G. M. Matthews, 'Impostor Phenomenon: Attributions for Success and Failure', paper presented at American Psychological Association, Toronto, 1984.
2. P. R. Clance, P.R., and S. A. Imes, S.A., (1978). 'The Impostor Phenomenon in High-achieving Women: Dynamics and Therapeutic interventions', Psychotherapy: Theory, Research and Practice, 15, 241–247.
3. P. Honey and A. Mumford (1982). Manual of Learning Styles. London: Peter Honey Associates.

PART ONE

What is Impostor Syndrome?

CHAPTER ONE

The Effects Of Impostor Syndrome

Case study: sabotaged by fear

At the age of thirty-one, Daniel was a successful lawyer. He had won a number of high-profile cases and been praised in the newspapers. People meeting him for the first time were struck by his confident, upbeat air and his dynamic energy. Here was a man who got things done well. Everyone agreed that he was 'going places'.

Daniel was headhunted for a top legal team at a prestigious London law firm. The team leader was especially delighted that Daniel had joined his team, and he was sure Daniel would make a valuable team member.

Most of Daniel's colleagues were second and third generation barristers. By contrast, Daniel had been raised in a poor family, from which he had been the only one to go to university. He was embarrassed by his strong northern accent and started to think that his background set him apart from the team. Daniel withdrew somewhat and didn't mix with the team socially.

His first team project was to research a point of law for a high-profile defence. The whole team was working flat out, scrutinising legal minutiae and past cases to find the best strategy. Daniel found an unusual and remarkable solution, which impressed the whole team. But when everyone congratulated him, he just said, 'I got lucky.' This appeared to be humility, and his boss was pleased that Daniel was such a good team player.

However, Daniel genuinely believed it was luck that he had found the solution, and luck that he had been hired for the job. He suspected that he didn't belong there. He was convinced that despite his position, his prior accomplishments and his recognition for outstanding work, someone would eventually realise they'd made a mistake in hiring him. Daniel was constantly looking over his shoulder, waiting for someone to accuse him of being a fraud, and he started to dread going to work every morning.

When he was asked for his written opinion on legal cases, Daniel could not bring himself to write what he actually thought. He was sure this would give him away as a fraud. Instead, he cut and pasted from textbooks, hoping it would sound plausible. While he knew this was not his best work, his anxiety won out over his conscientiousness.

As the stress continued to build, Daniel had a constant cold and was run down. He couldn't wait for the end of each day, then he would agonise over his work in the evening, sometimes waking up in the middle of the night panicking that he had made some terrible mistake.

Daniel did not mention his thoughts and feelings to anyone, in work or out of it. He kept up a cheerful attitude at work so that his boss and colleagues would not suspect what was really going on for him. This made him feel even more like a fraud as he was smiling on the outside, but had a permanent tense knot in his stomach.

Eventually, the anxiety became unbearable. After just two months in this top position, Daniel resigned. He felt it was better to leave before anyone discovered he was a fraud and save himself from the humiliation of being found out and fired.

Daniel spent three months completely burnt out and unable to work. He later did some part-time paralegal work and eventually started his own one-man family law firm. He has always regretted that his fear of failure ended a potentially spectacular legal career.

Daniel's experience is not unusual. Seven out of ten of your successful coaching clients experience impostor syndrome at some point. The effects include anxiety and stress, and can lead to addictions, burnout and quitting great careers.

As a coach, you can help. Impostor syndrome is not a lack of confidence or low self-esteem. Nor can it be helped by praise, which in some cases makes it worse. Learn the tools to help your client move through this difficult experience and go on to achieve spectacular results. It's all here in this guide.

Who does impostor syndrome affect?

When first documenting the phenomenon of impostor syndrome, Clance and Imes examined a group of female post-graduate students. These women described feelings of not belonging or deserving their place in the post-graduate programme. Each secretly believed that they had been admitted by accident, administrative error, because the admissions officer or professor was attracted to them, because they were simply lucky, or they'd had 'unfair' help. Every story was different, but the theme beneath each one was that the women believed they had somehow cheated the rigorous selection process. Consequently, they experienced a fear that at some point they would be found out and sent home in shame.

Initial studies showed that female students experienced impostor syndrome more than their male counterparts, and so researchers first thought it was a women's issue. This initial conclusion was due to the cultural issue of men not being accepted if they reveal thoughts or feelings of being 'weak', and so the men originally interviewed did not admit to such feelings. Later studies[4] conducted anonymously showed that impostor syndrome affects men and women equally. Compared to the 1970s, today's men are more likely to talk about their experience, but regardless of gender, impostor syndrome remains something that most people are reluctant to reveal.

Some people endure impostor feelings constantly, and use coping strategies such as addictions to get them through each day. For most, it sits around in the background and flares up when certain situations trigger it. More on this later.

It's important to note that I'm *not* referring to people who actually are frauds and have lied and cheated to get where they are in life. Instead, I'm referring to a false belief held by people who are perfectly capable and successful. No matter how good they are, or how successful they become, they are not convinced that's enough or that they deserve their success.

Impostor sufferers rarely feel like frauds in every area of their life. They don't feel like frauds when they're driving their car, for example. There tends to be a small number of activities in which they feel fraudulent. Like me with the leadership issue, they may have avoided these activities for many years. Often they underestimate their true capability because they expect perfection, so it's a faulty perception. Sometimes they have an unrecognised skills gap and simply need some training or mentoring. Whatever the reason, impostor sufferers are usually confused by the feeling that they're not good enough, particularly when they are used to being capable and comfortable in their work.

As you work with your client to uncover their impostor activity, you help them to understand their confusion. Once they have clarity, you can then plan how to help them move through it.

Coaching makes a difference

If Daniel had had a coach, and if that coach had known how to help him overcome impostor syndrome, then his career and life would look so different today.

If a person is suffering from impostor syndrome, simply talking to a coach about the experience has a huge benefit, getting them past the secrecy and denial, and reducing their sense of isolation. Building on that great start, a coach will explain the underlying cause of impostor syndrome to their client and how common it is. That eliminates any idea the client may have that it's just them, and puts an end to the confusion.

From there, the coach's work involves reducing anxiety and hypervigilance, and reframing situations, especially mistakes. The client's perfectionism can then diminish, and calm replaces stress.

Summary

In this chapter, we learned that impostor syndrome is more prevalent and more destructive than many people realise. Primarily, this is because sufferers have kept their feelings secret for fear of looking weak. However, impostor syndrome is not weakness, it is a normal response to core beliefs many people were taught in childhood which is triggered by certain circumstances. It can affect anyone. Coaches share a passion and drive to help people move through challenging circumstances and improve the quality and experience of their lives. By understanding impostor syndrome in depth, you will have a great opportunity to make a real difference to your clients.

Sometimes people are not aware of the problem themselves, and will need help recognising it. Sometimes they will want to keep it a secret from you – after all, they fear being found out as a fraud. Your ability to help them will rely on you identifying and defining the problem.

4. S. Fried-Buchalter. *Sex Roles,* December 1997, 37, Issue 11–12, 847–859.

CHAPTER 2

The Symptoms Of Impostor Syndrome

How do you spot someone with impostor syndrome when they tend to keep it secret? There are certain behaviours that give you a clue, and we'll look at the most common impostor behaviours in this chapter.

Your client might be reluctant to tell you how they feel for fear of your disapproval. Many others are unaware that their difficulties stem from impostor syndrome. And if your client has been referred to you by a manager, they may not trust your confidentiality. You often need to play the detective.

Characteristic impostor behaviours to look out for are:

- Perfectionism
- Deflection
- Comparing

- Secrecy
- Lying
- Hiding
- Avoiding
- Over-preparing
- Procrastinating
- Never having enough

Impostor behaviours appear as a group rather than one at a time. The combinations of behaviours are different for everyone.

Perfectionism

Some perfectionists are easy to spot. These are the perfectly groomed, immaculately turned out people who get overly upset when their clothes, hair, makeup, etc. become messy or dirty. They may extend their perfectionism to their possessions and the people they are linked to, e.g. their children and spouse.

Not all perfectionism is visual. People can be relaxed about their appearance and perfectionist about being right and knowledgeable. Similarly, they can be perfectionist about their work performance, fitness, or social interactions. The key to spotting perfectionism is to look for a client's intolerance of mistakes and flaws. The imperfection becomes an emotional drama.

Perfectionism is a common impostor behaviour. Often a client will agree with you that yes, logically, perfection is not a realistic goal. It is impossible for anyone to achieve. But somehow, the impossibility of that goal doesn't apply to *them*; they do need to be perfect.

Your client may justify their perfectionism as 'high standards' and consider it a virtue or an integral part of their personality. It's neither. High standards are something people work towards, but perfectionism is the need to be flawless, and anxiety follows when the perfectionist doesn't achieve it. The heart of perfectionism is the fear of making any mistakes at all.

Impostor sufferers will tend to ignore their successes and focus only on anything that is not perfect. They see what they have not accomplished and take that to mean they are not good enough, criticising themselves for any imperfections in their results. Then they fear that others will see their imperfect results and reject them for being a fraud.

When they have done well, perfectionists don't view the congratulations and accolades they receive as well-deserved. Instead, they believe that they have fooled every-one – for now. It's only a matter of time before the 'real' them is discovered.

One pattern of perfectionism is that a person will change jobs or employers every few years. In a new job, they have a perfect record because they have no history. As time goes by, mistakes inevitably creep in and they start to worry about being found out. As their anxiety builds, they feel increasingly uncomfortable at work until they move jobs.

Jumping from one position to another is not necessarily a problem. Indeed, it's a well-established career progression for high-achievers, who are expected to gain broad experi-ence in many roles. The difference between career progres-sion and impostor syndrome is the mounting discomfort someone feels the longer they stay in one position.

Deflecting

Many people feel uncomfortable when they're praised, and the impostor syndrome sufferer will experience this discomfort as a combination of not thinking they deserve the praise and pressure to repeat the success in the future. As a result, they discount and deflect praise, as we saw with Daniel in Chapter 1.

Deflecting is easy to test. When they're congratulated for a job well done, an impostor sufferer will frequently say phrases such as:

- Oh, anyone could have done it
- It was nothing really
- I just got lucky
- I had plenty of help
- It was just good timing

These comments sound like someone who is modest and polite, and usually get taken at face value. Indeed, a modest and polite person would say exactly the same things. It's not the words, but the feelings and beliefs that underlie them. For someone who is simply being modest, these casual phrases are an acknowledgement of the compliment and nothing more.

For someone who is feeling like a fraud, the deflecting phrases have a different meaning. 'Anyone could have done it' minimises the skill, time or effort they have put into the success. 'It was nothing really' minimises the challenge or complexity of the task. 'I just got lucky' is a sincere belief that the success was a fluke. They don't think they could repeat it. 'I had plenty of help' is a great phrase from someone recognising the support of their team and colleagues. However, some people are convinced that getting help is cheating, and therefore their contribution doesn't count. 'It was just good timing' again minimises the person's own skill, effort or talent, and puts their success down to random outside influences.

As these phrases are used by both impostor syndrome sufferers and modest people, how do we spot the impostor? If we were to carry on praising them, the modest people would politely concede that they did well, they're pleased with their accomplishment, they're glad you noticed, etc. However, impostor sufferers will move from one deflecting comment to another, never taking ownership of a job well done.

In fact, if we persist in praising them, they will become agitated, change the subject or make an excuse and leave. Although it makes their underlying beliefs clear, I don't recommend carrying on praising an impostor syndrome sufferer as it adds to their distress. Instead, notice this as a pattern that you may need to probe gently from time to time.

Comparing

Our society loves to compare, measure, and evaluate everything and everyone. Who is faster, stronger, smarter, prettier, wealthier – you name it, we compare it.

It's easy to measure simple things like height and weight, and objects like money and houses. It's harder to figure out social comparisons. For example, one person may have a large circle of casual friends, another a small group of close friends. Which group of friends is better? People have different preferences and personalities; a dream come true for one person may be a nightmare for another.

Impostor sufferers compare themselves with others, just as most people do. However, their comparison is distorted. They compare how other people *look* on the outside to how they themselves are *feeling* on the inside.

Have you ever seen a brilliant speaker captivate a room, calmly and confidently entertaining, then asked them later how it felt for them? Try it. If they're open, they may reveal their nervousness, where they had doubts or other negative emotions. We all tend to hide our innermost feelings, particularly on stage or at work.

Impostor sufferers forget that and take people at face value. They simplify other people's emotions and assume those people's inner feelings match their outer appearance. When their colleagues are high-achievers then the differences seem even greater. They find it hard to imagine that their brilliant colleagues are feeling any of the doubt and conflict that they are, because their colleagues look like they're doing so well. And of course, no-one is talking about their true feelings. An impostor sufferer thinks that they're the only one who is feeling like a fraud. Comparing makes them feel like they don't belong.

Daniel's family was ashamed of their poverty, an attitude which Daniel adopted. This attitude taught him that his background was not good enough, and by extension, neither was he.

Daniel's work colleagues had had very different experiences of childhood. The contrast between them was stark, and Daniel felt isolated as a result. He was naturally reluctant to share any of his childhood experiences with his new colleagues, increasing the separation he felt from them.

Secrecy

Secrecy is the hallmark of impostor syndrome. The fear of being found out means that sufferers don't tell people about how they are feeling. Unfortunately, this perpetuates the issue – nobody talks about it, so sufferers think they're the only ones feeling that way.

Daniel never revealed his reasons for leaving to his employer or work colleagues. None of them had any idea of his struggles. To them, he was a brilliant, talented lawyer. Daniel had not shared any of his feelings with his family or friends either, which is a classic symptom. Indeed, when I interviewed Daniel, he revealed that he had still not told his wife of ten years. That shows the level of shame he was feeling. Daniel tried to deal with it all himself, and consequently felt even more isolated, alone and unable to cope.

Lying

When he was three years old, Daniel was playing with his sister. He had carefully set down his cup of blackcurrant juice on one end of the sofa, and the two children were having a blast jumping up and down on the other end, followed by a game of chase outside.

They heard their mother shout from the living room, 'Who spilt juice on the sofa?'

Daniel's sister, two years older and wiser, promptly said, 'Not me,' and Daniel echoed that. The siblings then looked at the old dog lying innocently on the rug by the television.

'Well, don't leave cups on the sofa,' their mother grumbled and stomped off to the kitchen for a cloth.

At three years old, Daniel had learned to avoid anger, disapproval and punishment by lying. In fact, most people learn this lesson. Children are *told* that it's bad to lie, but are often *shown* that they can get away with less punishment or disapproval if they do lie. By their actions, parents teach their children to lie.

As people get older, they continue to lie about mistakes, hiding them, blaming others, being evasive or not mentioning them. People who feel like frauds especially dread having their mistakes discovered, as they consider it would prove to others that they are not good enough. So they conceal mistakes rather than bringing them out into the open.

Research[5] has shown that impostor sufferers are conscientious about their work and hold high standards, yet their perfectionism makes them feel they can never be conscientious enough. When they do eventually make a mistake, fear takes over. They know they should be honest, yet their fear of being found to be a fraud is greater than their desire to be transparent. Lying is a response to fear.

Hiding the mistake increases anxiety, too. Sufferers may lie awake at night worrying, and berate themselves for their error.

Lying is exacerbated if mistakes are punished at work rather than being used as learning experiences. A corporate environment of blame and scapegoating encourages people to lie, just as three-year-old Daniel learned to lie to avoid punishment for his mistake.

Hiding

People often resort to hiding their skills when they fear being discovered to be a fraud. At some point in their career, they suspect that they are out of their depth and they retreat. Of course, they have not suddenly become incapable; they have reached the limit of their belief that they are good enough to do the job.

People hide by not applying for or refusing promotion. They are not people who are naturally shy or have low self-esteem; they are highly successful, capable and confident. However, they think that the next step is too much of a risk. In this way, people can keep themselves small. To the rest of the world, they will appear successful, and people don't necessarily notice that they don't reach their potential. However, refusing promotion and not putting forward their true creative ideas reduces what they can accomplish.

Hiding can look like:

- Not speaking up in meetings and discussions
- Not revealing their actual thoughts and ideas
- Putting forward what they think others want to hear or expect

Impostor logic says that if an idea that is not the impostor sufferer's is criticised, then they have a level of distance from the criticism. It's a protective mechanism to prevent feeling bad about themselves.

In the case study in Chapter 1, Daniel put forward a made-up legal opinion as a way to hide his true point of view. Had anyone disagreed with his fabricated opinion, Daniel would have had some emotional insulation from the criticism. This was an entirely unconscious way to protect himself from being 'found' to be a phony.

What Daniel failed to see was the skill and talent it took to concoct a fake legal opinion. Even this level of work was considered good; he was never challenged on it. However, had Daniel written his actual opinion, his work could have been truly brilliant. His fear meant that he never reached his true potential as a lawyer in that company.

In this way, people can keep themselves small. To the

rest of the world they will already appear successful and people don't necessarily notice them not reaching greater potential. Refusing promotion and not putting forward their true creative ideas reduces what they can accomplish.

The world is diminished when great people play small.

Avoiding

Thirty per cent of high-achievers do not report that they feel like a fraud. I was one of these. However, it doesn't mean that 30% of high-achievers are necessarily feeling good enough about themselves. Some avoid situations that could trigger impostor syndrome. Typically, people in this group would refuse promotion or a new job as they would not want to risk 'failure'.

This was my experience of impostor syndrome when I joined a PhD programme rather than a fast-track management role. People can be completely unaware that they are avoiding difficult situations; it simply seems like they're making 'more interesting' choices, which was the case for me.

If people are doing routine jobs and not expanding their work horizons, then they can go a lifetime unconsciously avoiding a particular situation. For high-achievers, however, continued career success means that they are required to take on more responsibility and expand their range of activities. When this bumps up against their impostor activity – the task or role which makes them feel vulnerable if it's not performed perfectly – then impostor syndrome develops and stress increases, sometimes dramatically.

Others stay in one company despite feeling uncomfortable. They believe that they got into their job by mistake or good fortune or accident, and are convinced that no-one else would hire them if they tried to make a change.

Avoidance will show up in any area where someone feels they're not good enough, and that feeling drives their behaviour. This is a significant pain, particularly for high-achievers, as they are frustrated that they can't feel better about their impostor activity.

Over-preparing

Have you ever witnessed a team member showing up for a meeting with a huge stack of papers when they've only been asked for a simple report? That's a classic sign of over-preparing.

Impostor syndrome sufferers often deny that over-preparing is a problem. They consider themselves to be thorough and to have a good work ethic. Indeed, few workplaces would see it as a problem; a thorough job is the ideal. However, over-preparing and its close friend perfectionism come at a heavy price. There is a difference between appropriate effort for the task and working yourself into the ground to achieve a result. That much effort is unsustainable and easily leads to burnout and stress-related illness. It's not a long-term, balanced or healthy strategy.

It is a good work ethic to prepare well. However, over-preparing has a whole different feeling and drive. Over-preparing is driven by anxiety. People may experience this anxiety as dread or feeling overwhelmed when they're given a new project, anticipating how much it is going to cost in time and effort.

In the context of impostor syndrome, we need to explore the reason why over-preparing happens. A great question to ask clients is 'What would happen if you didn't prepare so much?' The answer to this question usually shows their underlying fear or worry. Sometimes it's about being the most knowledgeable person in the room. Sometimes the issue is more around the fear of making a mistake. In either situation, the fear of not being good enough drives the behaviour.

Procrastinating

Procrastination is the opposite of overworking, although some people can combine the two. Procrastination is not an obvious symptom of impostor syndrome, unlike perfectionism. There are many reasons why people procrastinate, but the impostor version is distinctive.

Impostors will put off a project until the last minute. They will then work late into the night to complete it, quite possibly over-preparing, too. This work will be stressful and driven by a fear of failure.

As the impostor is genuinely a high-achieving and competent person, the presentation will often go well. However, they won't feel pleased about their work. They will think that they have fooled everyone and got lucky again. So instead of feeling satisfied at a job well done, they still feel like a fraud. They also believe that they might not be so lucky next time, so the anxiety persists.

If the presentation goes badly and the impostor syndrome sufferer is criticised, that does not feel so bad to them. Of course, they don't enjoy the criticism, but they have the internal excuse that it was a rushed job and so it's not a criticism of their true abilities. This is the protective aspect of procrastination, and tends to be the feeling behind it.

Bear in mind that people are often unaware of these thoughts. More likely they are confused or frustrated that they procrastinated in the first place.

Never having enough

One less visible symptom of impostor syndrome is never having enough. For example, a sufferer may believe they never have enough qualifications, money, companies or material possessions.

Case study: never enough

Peter was a highly valued freelance troubleshooter in business-critical systems. He had many qualifications and was great at his work. However, Peter always had the feeling that if he could just get one more qualification, then he would finally feel comfortable and people would recognise he was good enough to do the job. His customers already valued his work, and he had an impressive list of enthusiastic testimonials. This demonstrates that praise does not register or help with impostor syndrome.

Peter had grown up in a competitive household with two older brothers. His father made it clear that their academic achievement was important to him, and his approval and disapproval was related to his sons' performance.

Peter drifted through school, not applying himself much, but got a good university degree nonetheless.

Peter got his first job with the normal discomfort of a new environment, new things to learn and expectations from his colleagues and boss. He felt the need to prove himself, and fell back on his father's teaching that more qualifications would help. So he rushed out to get himself certified, and has spent a small fortune on his training over the years.

Of course, the problem is not a lack of qualifications. Peter is trying to feel better emotionally, and believes that more qualifications will solve the problem.

Many people believe that more money will cure their discomfort. While money will solve practical problems and make life easier, it doesn't help emotionally. This is why we see a classic pattern of a wealthy person working hard to get their next million, ten million, and then billion. Each time, it's never enough. They're still emotionally uncomfortable, but their thinking is stuck in the rut that the solution must be more money.

As a coach, you are able to help break clients out of that mental rut.

Summary

Impostor sufferers display many kinds of behaviours. This can make it hard to spot, and secrecy adds to the difficulty. The common thread in impostors' behaviours is the underlying thought that they're a fraud, and if others find out then things will go badly wrong.

We have looked at the range of impostor behaviours in this chapter and gained insight into the thought patterns that create them. By noting these behaviours in your client, you can build a picture of the level of their stress.

Many times, impostor sufferers will downplay the anxiety or discomfort they're experiencing. This can be a denial of the problem or a reluctance to admit something that they think makes them appear weak. However, impostor feelings are highly destructive and can have a substantial impact on your client's wellbeing. Chapter 3 describes the extent of this stress to help you address the issue fully and improve the quality of your client's life.

5. B. Wille, M. Feys, F. De Fruyt, and F. Anseel, (2014). 'Fear of Being Exposed: The Trait-Relatedness of the Impostor Phenomenon and its Relevance in the Work Context', Journal of Business and Psychology 30: 565–581.

CHAPTER 3

The Pain Of Impostor Syndrome

It is easy to underestimate the damaging effects of impostor syndrome since it is a stress that sufferers keep hidden as much as possible. However, the anxiety of it, which builds over time, has significant effects on health, emotional state and work performance. Sufferers may require time off for recuperation. The anxiety can lead to burnout if people try to push through it. They may feel overwhelmed and depressed, even suicidal. Sometimes the stress of the situation is so intense that they give up and quit their jobs completely.

Typical negative effects of impostor syndrome include:

- Anxiety
- Isolation
- Stress-related illness
- Burnout

- Pushing through
- Addictions
- Reduced performance
- Depression
- Giving up
- Volatile behaviour

Anxiety

Anxiety is the dominant emotion of impostor syndrome, due to the sufferer's fear of being found not to be good enough, and their anticipation of the rejection and humiliation that discovery will cause. They have a persistent sense of 'waiting for the hammer to fall' – that at any moment, someone will be standing over them, calling them a fraud. The constant background tension creates hypervigilance.

Anxiety is compounded by the sufferer's self-judgment when they do make a mistake. Rather than treat it as a learning experience in a calm manner, they berate themselves for the mistake in the moment. They return to that mistake and replay it over again, much like someone with a sore tooth continually poking at it with their tongue, feeling the pain long after the event.

Mistakes can subconsciously haunt people with impostor

syndrome, and they wake up with a jolt in the middle of the night, remembering the mistake and feeling shame or fear. As sufferers focus on their mistakes, it makes it hard for them to move on. It also makes their mistakes seem bigger and more significant than they are.

Isolation

Isolation was recently described by the US Surgeon General as the 'greatest public health crisis'.[6] Isolation leads to stress, which is a significant contributor to fatal illness.

Isolation is a result of the modern lifestyle, where young people typically move away from families for work, and more marriages end in divorce. A greater proportion of people are living alone than at any other time in history. However, biologically and socially, we are still tribal beings. Historically, the survival of the human race depended on children being cared for, and the tribe working together for food and protection.

People with impostor feelings have a sense that they don't belong in their work 'tribe' or group. This automatically makes them feel isolated. The worst punishment in prehistoric times was ejection from the tribe, which would have led to certain death, and 'on the outside' is still a scary place to be. The fear of being found out to be a fraud – and therefore ejected from the group – taps into the impostor sufferer's primal fear.

Isolation increases when they compare their inner feelings to their colleagues' outward success. This causes them to believe that they are the only one who feels this way, and this apparent difference adds to their sense of isolation and reinforces their belief that they don't belong. Furthermore, as they keep their feelings a secret, their isolation increases.

Stress-related illness

Anxiety, hypervigilance and isolation cause stress hormones to be continually released within the impostor syndrome sufferer's body and their blood pressure to rise. In the short-term, this stress causes frequent illness and exhaustion, and they feel overwhelmed. In the long-term, critical stress-related illnesses occur, including heart problems and immune system disorders.

Only when an impostor syndrome sufferer's body succumbs to stress-related illnesses are they forced to take time off for recovery.

Burnout

As impostor feelings drive people to achieve more or do things better (i.e. perfectly), overworking becomes common. They ignore their bodies' needs for rest, balance, exercise, sleep and good nutrition. While anyone can achieve plenty with a brief, huge spurt of effort, it is not a sustainable, long-term strategy.

Fear-driven overworking and neglect of their bodies' natural needs frequently lead impostor sufferers to burnout. Unlike a stress-related illness, burnout tends to have a stronger emotional component – sufferers are not only physically exhausted, but mentally and emotionally overloaded, too.

Being over-sensitive and emotionally on-edge is an extra level of stress, bringing them closer to emotional exhaustion.

Pushing through

The fear of making mistakes – which sufferers imagine will prove them worthless – means that they work in a fear-driven way. Work develops a sense of urgency, and they approach it tensely, sometimes with a feeling of dread. Challenges appear as threats to be overcome and not projects that will be fun and test their skills.

Being driven to succeed is often seen as a good thing in high-achievers. However, 'driven' often means driven by fear of failure, public ridicule or not being good enough. People are so used to being driven by fear that it is seen as normal, and indeed sometimes fear of failure appears necessary in order to be successful. Culturally, men tend to be encouraged to ignore their feelings, grit their teeth and suffer any pain in order to get the job done, so they may be more prone to this effect of impostor syndrome.

If a person's reason for discomfort is purely a skills gap, then learning what they need to learn as quickly as possible is a good way to pull through it. However, it does not work for the impostor syndrome sufferer because a skills gap is not the underlying cause of their discomfort. The cause is their belief that they are not good enough, as we shall see later. If this is not addressed, the emotional stress gets bottled up and builds until it blows or they collapse – the classic burnout situation.

Addictions

Extensive study[7] identifies stress and isolation as major factor in addictions. People turn to addictive substances, such as alcohol, drugs, tobacco, or foods, and addictive behaviours, such as gambling, work, shopping, sex, watching porn, or extreme sports, to try and numb themselves from emotional pain. Behavioural addictions also include social behaviours such as anger, bullying and victimhood. In fact, any activity can become addictive if it is used to avoid discomfort.

If someone tries to give up an addictive behaviour they've been using to cope with stress, they often replace it with another addiction. Impostor syndrome sufferers can bounce between different addictions for years without addressing the underlying cause.

It's useful to make a note of the number and extent of your coaching clients' addictions; anywhere they feel their behaviour is compulsive or a little 'out of control'. By escaping or numbing their feelings with addictive behaviours, they often do not perceive the problem as being so severe and may think they are doing better than they really are.

Reduced performance

Human physiology changes when people are anxious. Their vision narrows from a peripheral view to a tunnel-like focus on the object of their fear. This is a healthy reaction to a fast-moving snake, but in a work environment it makes people less mentally flexible and creative, and more resistant to change and growth. Ironically, this lowers their performance on the job.

Depression

Depression has several causes, including imbalances in body chemistry or emotions, and chronic negative thinking. For impostor sufferers, depression can be a consequence of isolation, feeling overwhelmed and anxiety, and the thinking behind them.

Giving up

When stress gets to a crisis point, impostor sufferers often find they have only one way to relieve it: quitting. This may mean quitting their position but remaining in the same company, or leaving the company, or sometimes giving up on their career entirely.

If a sufferer sees quitting their job or career as shameful or failure, then the prospect will keep them working until the stress becomes unbearable. This is often where burnout is reached. But some can't face the perceived public humiliation of failure, and their way out is suicide.

Volatile behaviour

By continually watching out for 'discovery', impostor sufferers become more sensitive to criticism and are likely to misinterpret neutral comments. They may become either defensive and prickly to those around them or withdrawn, depending on their habitual way of reacting to criticism.

Effects of impostor syndrome on business

The consequences of impostor behaviours are also felt by the business. If the sufferer is absent because of stress-related illness, burnout, depression or addiction, then their work needs to be done by others on the team, which means the company is not achieving its full potential. It loses opportunities, particularly if that individual was in a leadership role. The leadership vacuum will hinder projects and operations.

If the impostor sufferer quits their job, then recruiting a replacement will cost time and money, as will the replacement's training. The business will also have lost a highly valuable member of the team who could otherwise have contributed greatly.

Is the solution for businesses to hire people who don't

experience impostor syndrome? That's not feasible as the problem affects so many high-achievers, and triggers can set it off unpredictably. A wise business leader will work through the guidelines for coaches detailed in Part 3 of this book. By implementing these guidelines, they will not only reduce the risk of triggering impostor syndrome, they will also develop top performing teams to achieve remarkable results.

Effects on colleagues

Sufferers naturally keep impostor syndrome a secret from others, especially their work colleagues. Therefore, co-workers and bosses will be unaware that someone is suffering, though the sufferer's impostor syndrome may affect them in other ways.

If they are unwilling to risk putting their ideas forward, then the team misses out on their input, creativity and participation. If they tend to isolate themselves, then the team is not a cohesive unit with all members fully engaged. The whole team is diminished by that. As their stress and anxiety build, the sufferer may develop addictions or volatile behaviour. This will generate conflict, leading to a less harmonious team and lower morale.

Sufferers will tend to hide any mistakes that they have made, making joint projects vulnerable. Rather than being discussed and resolved, the mistakes come to light as a surprise, creating more problems.

The quality of a top-notch team will be reduced by the impostor sufferer not playing to their full capabilities. Lost opportunities due to the sufferer's lack of input mean that the team will not achieve the excellence they all want. As the impostor sufferer is still good and capable, their performance will rarely stand out as being deficient. However, there is a level of excellence they cannot achieve because of the distraction and stress of their anxiety.

Is this coaching?

Where do we draw the line with coaching? People may have mild stress symptoms or severe anxiety and burnout when you meet them. At what point do their symptoms need a psychotherapist or medical professional?

There are so many different types of coaches and coaching situations that you need to decide for yourself what issues you are happy to address. You can only achieve this definition when you are clear on what you are qualified for and willing to do. But no matter how well-defined the scope of your coaching, you will likely get people coming to you needing help that you are unwilling to provide. Sometimes this will be clear from your first meeting, and you can refer them to someone more suited to their situation immediately. Other times, a client may be unaware of the underlying issue and it will only surface after a few coaching sessions.

For example, a financial coach may have a client who presents financial issues as their problem. Then the coach may discover after a while that their client's issue is actually a relationship problem, and they need a relationship counsellor or coach. If you decide any work is beyond your remit, the best policy is to be clear and honest with your client and refer them elsewhere. For this reason, it's great to build a network of coaches and support systems. And of course, others in your network can refer people to you for your area of expertise.

Case study: avoiding the issue

Sometimes people may come to you for coaching because they don't want to address their real issue, possibly out of fear or denial. In my work as a transformational coach, I help clients make big changes and grow in many areas: mental, emotional and spiritual. Consequently, I see a broad range of issues.

In her initial consultation, one woman revealed to me that her doctor had referred her to a psychiatrist for assessment for possible schizophrenia. This was definitely beyond my skills and qualifications, and so she would not become my client. But I decided to spend the hour with her and try to be of some service. I could equally have ended the consultation and refunded her money.

She was terrified of the potential diagnosis of schizophrenia and wanted me to say her issue was actually a spiritual one. I always start by looking for the most simple and practical explanations, which means that spiritual issues are last on the list. So we just discussed her experiences.

She was having strong hallucinations and severe obstructive sleep apnoea (waking up suddenly unable to breathe). Extreme sleep deprivation can cause hallucinations. Sleep apnoea may be a cause and/or symptom of schizophrenia, which researchers are still exploring.[8]

I explained that I was not qualified to make any medical or psychiatric diagnosis, which would be illegal as well as unethical. I did, however, confirm hers was not a spiritual issue. She still refused to see the psychiatrist out of fear, so we made a plan she could live with – she would go to the local sleep clinic and explore the sleep apnoea.

We then looked at some possible outcomes: her issue might be sleep apnoea and require medication or surgery, or it might indeed be schizophrenia. And if it was schizophrenia then she would need the best help possible, which would be psychiatric care. By this time, she was calm enough to accept the possibility of a diagnosis of schizophrenia and that there was help available to her if that was the case.

What had I done as a coach? I'd listened without judgement and not dismissed her fears, which was helpful in itself. I'd given her a practical step to help her establish what was going on. Many people are afraid when they feel trapped, and choices help people relax. I was also honest with her that a schizophrenia diagnosis was a possibility, but I modelled not being afraid of the diagnosis or making it a drama, which helped her do the same.

Coaches encounter all sorts of situations. It's useful to have a basic knowledge of potential issues so that we have an idea of how we can realistically offer help when it is outside of our remit. This applies equally to impostor syndrome and its severity.

Mental health basic training

Coaching training courses are not standardised and vary in their content and expectations. Some people become coaches without formal training, especially in life coaching, or based on specialist experience like business mentoring. Regardless of our training and experience, we always have the possibility of a client revealing issues like schizophrenia or suicidal thoughts. The best we can do, as the Girl Guide motto says, is 'Be prepared'.

One such training programme for coaches is the Mental Health First Aid (MHFA) training course,[9] which gives you a framework to follow when your clients are struggling. You then know exactly when to refer them to a medical professional. You can then have confidence that you are being of genuine help in any situation that may arise.

If you are coaching within an organisation, then establishing volunteer MHFAs similar to regular volunteer first aid schemes, will provide a level of support for the whole workforce. Potential problems will be more likely to be caught early on, when they are far more manageable and treatable.

Impostor syndrome stress

Impostor syndrome is not a recognised psychiatric disorder and does not need referral to a psychotherapist. We will look at the false belief at the heart of impostor syndrome in Part 2 and how coaches can help in Part 3.

However, as we have seen in this chapter, the range of negative responses to impostor syndrome is large. Your first move depends upon the level of stress that your client is experiencing.

If they are in crisis, experiencing severe anxiety, burnout, severe addictions or suicidal thoughts, refer them to their doctor. A medical doctor can sign them off work and give them some time and space to recuperate. Your degree of involvement once they are out of crisis is up to you.

If clients are heavily stressed but not in crisis, you can review their situation and identify the triggers that may be making things worse. Common triggers are outlined in Chapter 4. You can then help them make some immediate changes to alleviate the anxiety. From there, the guidelines in this book will give them substantial relief from impostor feelings. This is also the case for chronic lower-level stress. Chronic impostor feelings are not to be ignored, though, because certain things can trigger a more intense experience, which may later lead to a crisis situation.

Summary

Impostor syndrome has many damaging stress effects. You may see them individually or combined. Sometimes everything will seem to be fine until you find your client relying on addictive behaviours to try and cope.

You can significantly reduce your client's stress by making them fully aware of it and helping them to come out of denial around destructuve coping behaviours. Knowing that theirs is a real problem can give your client the motivation to tackle it, with your assistance.

Your client will probably be confused about their impostor feelings, and may find myths on the internet which will add helplessness to their confusion. Your next step is to help them understand what they are experiencing and why. We will discuss the myths and real cause of impostor syndrome in the next chapter, helping you bring your clients much-needed clarity.

6. 19th US Surgeon General Vice Admiral Vivek Murthy, interview with Soledad O'Brien, Matter of Fact, broadcast 18 June 2016.

7. G. Baer (2010). Real Love and Post-Childhood Stress Disorder, Rome, GA: Blue Ridge Press.

8. Beth Israel Deaconess Medical Centre, 'Insight into Sleep's Role in Schizophrenia Offers Potential Treatment Path', 18 October 2016, ScienceDaily.com.

9. www.mhfaengland.org

CHAPTER 4

Understanding Impostor Syndrome

Impostor syndrome is a confusing experience for high-achievers. They're successful people, and often they've been fine until something triggers impostor behaviour. Suddenly, they feel anxious about being found out to be a fraud, but they don't know why. Or they may only see their anxiety and are baffled as to what is causing it.

This confusion is frustrating, too – they can't fix a problem they can't see. So it leads to them feeling helpless, another unpleasant emotion.

In this chapter, we will review common impostor syndrome myths – what it is not. We'll also explore the underlying cause, the two triggers for impostor syndrome, and situations that exacerbate the problem. This information alone can be such a relief to your coaching client, who will then know what's really going on, that they're not alone, and that you can help them.

Myths and reality

The issue of impostor syndrome is becoming more widely known, which is wonderful because people learn it's not just them suffering. Although it has now been identified and well documented, though, the underlying cause is still not well known. Myths have grown up about what it is and how to address it.

There are three myths about impostor syndrome:

- It's a lack of confidence
- It's low self-esteem
- It's incompetence

None of these is true. However, if your client suspects that the myths are true, it gives them another source of stress.

Case study: confidence and competence

When I was in my twenties, I climbed Mount Snowdon, the highest mountain in Wales. It didn't involve a rock climb with ropes and picks, just a scramble climb here and there.

This was my first climb, and my experienced friend explained the route and the type of climbing we'd be doing.

I felt confident. I'm certainly able to scramble, and I was fit enough to spend a few hours climbing, so I didn't have a lack of competence. We set out with all the right gear. The weather was cloudy, which was perfect because it wasn't too hot.

We climbed without incident until we got to 20 metres below the summit. Here the ground was a little unstable and some slate shingles started slipping under my feet. I was on the edge of my comfort zone, but I was still OK. It was a challenge, but I climbed half way up this shingle slope with a smile on my face.

Then, as I glanced down, the clouds parted. The large lake at the base of Mount Snowdon looked tiny. We were very high up, and I don't like heights. I froze in place; I could not go on.

Had I stopped being competent? No, I was still completely capable of getting to the top. Had I lost confidence that I could do the climb? No, I was still confident that I was able to climb, even on the tricky slate shingles.

The difference was now my fear of heights had been triggered. This is the distinction – nothing had changed, but a fear had come up.

This is what happens with impostor syndrome. People are doing well in their careers, meeting challenges. They regularly go outside their comfort zone and succeed. They are competent and confident. Then, a certain role or challenge comes up – their impostor activity – and it triggers fear. It's not a fear of not being competent, as they are competent; it's a fear of not being good *enough*, usually in one particular activity. The anxiety can be debilitating, as we saw in Daniel's story in Chapter 1.

Similarly, the problem is not low self-esteem. We're talking about high-achievers who are still capable and get results. In other parts of their lives, they have high self-esteem, and they may even concede they do a good job in the activity that creates the anxiety. It's just they don't feel good *enough*.

Impostor activity

Impostor syndrome strikes capable people in certain activities only, and they have learned to associate their worth with these activities. They believe that if they do well then they're worthy, and if they make mistakes or fail in this situation, they are unworthy, unlovable, and will be rejected and humiliated.

Every individual has different patterns of activities they associate with their worth. The difference depends on their upbringing, their natural talents, and what their parents, teachers or peers valued, praised or criticised.

Case study: relative values

Joy did not sing well, but she enjoyed a good karaoke. The reason she could sing comfortably with others watching is that she never believed that her singing skills meant anything about her. When people do not tie their worth to something, then they are free to enjoy the experience for what it is, whether they do it well or not.

Contrast this with Alex, who grew up in a musical family. His parents and siblings all played many instruments, sang beautifully, and valued music and musical ability. Alex was a little tone deaf, and although he sang well enough for most people, he didn't sing well by the standards of his family. And so he came to believe that his singing was not good enough. Specifically, he unconsciously thought that because he couldn't sing perfectly, he was not good enough. He became anxious when he thought about singing in public, and so he avoided it, despite the fact that friends told him he sang well. Alex discounted their comments and continued to feel that he was not good enough to sing in public.

Even though Alex was a better singer than Joy, the prospect of singing in front others was a nightmare for him.

It's all about what people tie their worth to. Individual values by which sufferers measure their worth include:

- Knowledge
- Qualifications
- Being right
- Intelligence
- Leadership
- Finances
- Creativity
- Mathematical ability
- Attractiveness

The list is endless.

Case study: social awkwardness

Jason grew up with a single mother and two sisters, thinking that he should always be confident, entertaining and charming in social situations. But he wasn't. There was nothing obvious in his childhood that would explain this social awkwardness; the underlying cause of impostor syndrome is not one traumatic event, as people sometimes believe. This added to Jason's confusion, as he couldn't spot where things had 'gone wrong'.

Anytime he made a social mistake, said the wrong thing or got a negative reaction, he felt embarrassed and ashamed. Without being aware of it, he subconsciously felt like he was not good enough. He had zero tolerance for his social mistakes.

Jason compared himself to other men whom he saw as more skilled socially. With the classic narrow focus of impostor syndrome, he ignored the evidence that other men sometimes made off comments or social gaffes, and he focused on their successes. He compared the outward appearance of their smooth charm to the turmoil he felt inside just thinking about social errors.

Jason's coping strategy became to avoid social situations entirely. He started his own business in web design and IT services, interacting with his customers by email, and was comfortable working that way for fifteen years. He was successful in his work, but never applied for awards that he would easily have won because he was so uncomfortable in a group setting.

Finally, he decided to expand his business, for which he needed a higher public profile and to attend networking events and industry awards. That was when he started to experience anxiety and feeling like a fraud.

This is typical of impostor syndrome. People may spend years avoiding a particular activity, but their success means they eventually have to engage in it. They then start to feel the anxiety of not being good enough.

Often people are not aware of what's going on and act on stressed feelings unconsciously. As we saw in Chapter 3, Peter knew that he didn't need more qualifications, yet he still felt that he would feel better if he got just one more certificate. Jason thought he had been inspired by a great business idea, which it was, but he was unaware he had chosen the perfect business to avoid social interactions.

It's common for impostor sufferers to experience stress and anxiety without being aware of the underlying cause. This lack of awareness adds to the confusion they feel around the stress, and increases discomfort.

The cause

Society reinforces a false belief that our worth as a human is conditional – our inherent value depends on what we say and do. We learn this in childhood, and it forms a foundational belief from which we operate.

Impostor syndrome occurs when people are doing the activity to which they attach their worth – the impostor activity – and worry that they're not good enough; that others will see their lack of perfection and judge them to be a fraud. There are ways to rewrite that original belief of conditional worth.[10] [11] The principles of these programmes are highly effective, and described in later chapters so that coaches can use them to help their clients resolve the issue.

In addition to the impostor activity, there are two major triggers that can spark an incidence of impostor syndrome: change and a critical environment.

Trigger 1: change/challenge

Top performers experience impostor feelings more than other people. The reason is that high-achievers tend to do a greater variety of tasks and fill a greater range of roles than the general population. When somebody becomes successful, it is natural that they will be asked to do more and more.

As high-achievers do a greater range of tasks, they are more likely to encounter an activity that they attach their worth to. It's often the thing they've been avoiding, and now they're in a situation where it is their next career step. And the fear of being seen to fail mounts quickly.

Consider a baker who has been baking bread and cakes for the past thirty years. Tomorrow he is going to be using the same methods as he has used all his life. He has all the skills he needs to do this work well, and he is unlikely to encounter any challenge to his baking skills.

If the same baker decides to enter a national baking competition and needs to invent some fabulous new recipes or techniques, then he may develop impostor syndrome triggered by this challenge. Bear in mind that it will only be a problem if he attaches his worth to baking the new recipes perfectly.

For successful business people, a new position is typically more complex and requires a greater skillset than they've used before. This can mean they will have to use different skills, such as people skills versus technical expertise. They will feel the pressure to perform at a high level while learning on the job. If they have been avoiding using these skills in the past, then they will lack experience while dreading looking less than perfect.

Trigger 2: critical environment

The second trigger for impostor syndrome is a critical environment, in which any mistakes people make are met with disapproval.

For people who work in the creative arts – authors,

actors, performers, musicians and painters – critique is normal. There are professional critics whose sole job is to pass judgment upon the work presented. Does this mean that all artists are plagued by impostor syndrome? Not at all, although it is common enough that highly successful artists will recognise it in themselves or in fellow artists.

Most artists will tell you that you need to have a thick skin to make it, because there will always be someone who doesn't like your work. The difference is what the artist makes the criticism *mean* about them as a person and their worth. If an artist ties their worth to the approval of critics then they will be in for a very stressful career.

The same situation arises in business, where a critical work environment in which blame, scapegoating, shouting and bullying are present can be a trigger. The sufferer already believes that they don't perform well enough in one activity, and they unconsciously look out for confirmation that their belief is true, while fearing it at the same time. A critical environment ramps up their anxiety around making mistakes and failing, and increases the stress and perceived consequences of them.

Disapproval of mistakes may not necessarily be loud or an obvious punishment. It can be expressed more subtly through rolling eyes, a sigh, slumping shoulders or an expression of disappointment. Sometimes a pointed silence is enough. Though these are quieter signs of disapproval, they still clearly convey that the person who has made the mistake is being judged as not good enough. This is enough to be a trigger.

The underlying theme of a critical work environment is that mistakes are personal failures not to be tolerated. As high-achievers reach more senior positions in whatever field they work in, they face an implicit raising of standards and expected performance, too. Often the result is that they view mistakes as forbidden.

Intensifiers

Certain situations exacerbate impostor feelings, including isolation and external stress. The female postgraduate students in Clance and Imes's original study of impostor syndrome were in a traditionally male environment. In the late 1970s, the number of female and male undergraduate students was about equal, but just twenty years previously, men had outnumbered women by two to one.[12] Postgraduate studies were still more male-dominated.

When most of the mothers of these female postgrads were young in the 1950s, common cultural thinking in the

West was that a woman went to university to find a good husband. Women's education was often considered less important than men's. This meant that the postgraduate women in the 1970s were going against the norm their parents had grown up with, and unconsciously passed on to them. This created a sense of not belonging, which increased the tension they felt.

Women in business and leadership roles are rare within some companies, so if an executive woman has impostor feelings, the old-fashioned cultural hint that they don't really belong in a leadership role will add to the stress, consciously or unconsciously. This same isolation can arise for anyone in a minority at work.

To our society's credit, we have been working to address inequality in the workplace regarding gender, race and disability, and more recently sexual orientation. Diversity policies exist in many companies, encouraging the management teams to reverse the old cultural bias. Ironically, though, whenever someone is in the minority, they may suspect they weren't hired on their merits but to fill some quota, feeding the 'I don't belong' idea. Even a hint that this may be the case can add fuel to the fire of impostor syndrome.

Feelings of not belonging can also result from other differences, including:

- Age differences, such as a young manager leading a team of older people or vice versa
- Different regional backgrounds and accents
- Differences in the wealth and experiences of people's childhoods
- Old-fashioned attitudes of class

We saw three of these in Daniel's case, all compounding the effect of his impostor syndrome.

Other intensifiers include lack of support at home (whether the sufferer is living alone or not) and additional stress from outside work, e.g. family or health problems.

Summary

Impostor syndrome is not a lack of confidence, incompetence or low self-esteem. It stems from a core belief people acquire in childhood that their worth as a human depends on their actions and how well they perform. Typically, impostor syndrome sufferers make certain activities representative of their worth and believe that they should excel or even be perfect at them.

Impostor feelings can be triggered by a challenging change or a critical environment. Intensifiers such as isolation and lack of support increase the stress.

When you can describe the cause and triggers of impostor syndrome, you give your clients the gift of understanding why they're struggling. This alone brings huge relief because the cause of the problem has been identified, and from there you can plan how to resolve it. Importantly, your client learns that this is not a personal flaw or failing, which helps them release any self-judgments. This reduces stress in itself and makes your client more open to practical solutions.

Part 1 covered what impostor syndrome is, what it looks like and its effects. We have also explored the myths and what triggers an episode. Now we need to understand the fundamental cause, which is the focus for Part 2. Once you know the whole problem, then you can address it fully and support your clients powerfully.

10. G. Baer, (2003). Real Love, Rome, GA: Blue Ridge Press.

11. T. Halliday, https://www.completesuccess.co.uk

12. C. T.Clotfelter, R. G. Ehrenberg, M, Getz, and J. J. Siegfried (1991). Economic Challenges In Higher Education, University of Chicago Press.

PART TWO

The
Success Frame

CHAPTER 5

The Underlying Cause

Impostor syndrome is caused by a belief in conditional worth – that our worth as a person depends upon what we do or don't do. This belief causes sufferers to fail to achieve their highest potential.

The problem of conditional worth was first studied in the 1950s by Dr Carl Rogers,[13] who is one of the founding fathers of clinical psychology. He identified conditional worth as a lack of congruence between who people believe themselves to be and who they truly are. They buy into a lie that they are not innately good enough and have to earn their worth somehow.

The problem of conditional worth

When we think our worth is conditional, we need to prove

ourselves worthy by constantly doing the 'right thing'. If we believe we are not good enough as we are, then we feel a combination of alone, empty, unlovable and worthless. We are vulnerable to a threat that our senses cannot detect; an emotional pain as real as any physical injury.

Rather than feeling that emotional pain, we link our worth to our actions. The activities we tie our worth to are as individual as we are. We may feel approval because of our success, looks, musical abilities, athleticism, intelligence, possessions, popularity, or thousands of other things. However, the pattern is the same for everyone – there are some areas in our lives where we think we must prove ourselves to be worthy.

Conditional worth is taught to us by parents, teachers, peers – it is a cultural lie that exists in every society in the world, and it is reinforced throughout our childhood and into our adult lives. We perpetuate this false belief by the way in which we view ourselves and understand our identity.

Creating core beliefs

Our childhood experience is incredible. Infants learn how to operate in the world and explore strategies for getting what they need to survive. Children make over one million new neuronal connections every second in order to build an accurate picture of the world, learning through observation, experimenting and repetition. They formulate beliefs about how the world works – thoughts and concepts that they habituate so that they can put much of their day-to-day life on autopilot. This autopilot allows people to reserve their attention and thinking for solving new problems and responding to crises. It is key to the success of our species.

Gravity is an excellent physical example of habituated thinking and action. We first learn to walk by falling down a lot, and we learn to adapt our movements to the Earth's gravitational pull. We act within the framework of gravity, but rarely do we consciously think about it. Unless we become astronauts and walk on other planets, then we need never review our internalised information about gravity.

Core beliefs are the mental equivalent of gravity. They are concepts that we hold to be so fundamentally true that we operate from their framework without conscious thought. Most of the time, we are not aware of our core beliefs explicitly. We usually need someone else to point out the implicit assumptions on which our worldview rests.

Our beliefs are created explicitly through direct teaching from society. They are also created implicitly; children observe behaviour, look for patterns and draw conclusions about what they mean. Children learn through daily repetition which beliefs are 'true', i.e. appear to be constant. Once the brain has identified 'truth', it operates from that framework without question.

As our reasoning becomes more sophisticated and we learn more, we build a database of experiences in our minds. Our choices are based on the solutions we can come up with, within the confines of what we believe to be true about ourselves and the world.

The 'truth' of conditional worth is, in fact, a lie. Only one in 100,000 people grow up with a belief in their unconditional worth.[14] It is not a question of whether we hold this belief. The questions are only how it is expressed and what impact it has on our lives.

How children develop conditional worth

Our biological goal as young children is to learn how to survive. We are completely dependent upon the goodwill and cooperation of our parents and wider society for everything we need. Anything that threatens our parental care is a threat to our very lives.

As young babies intently scanning our parents' faces, we learn that their expressions are not constant. We learn that some things we do will generate smiles and closeness, and other things we do will generate frowns, tension and maybe anger. When we are quiet, kind, obedient, tidy, etc., we tend to get the smiles and closeness. However, when we are noisy, upset, disobedient, dirty, etc., the smiles and closeness disappear.

Our conclusion as children is that the care of our parents (our survival) depends on how we behave. It is not enough to be ourselves; we need their approval in order to survive. We conclude that our worth depends on what we do.

Global culture has conditional worth built into it. Parents were taught this same core belief when they were children. Without instructions or examples on how to do it differently, parents simply perpetuate this belief.

No blame

At this point, you may be wondering if I am blaming parents, teachers and society as a whole for bringing children up with a sense of conditional worth. Not at all. In order to bring up a child with a sense of unconditional worth, parents need to have a sense of their own unconditional worth. If they don't have it, they can't give it to their children.

To illustrate this, pick a language you don't know. I'll use Japanese as an example. I don't speak Japanese because nobody taught me Japanese. My parents didn't teach me Japanese because they didn't know how to speak Japanese, either. They caused me not to know how to speak Japanese, but only because they didn't know how to themselves. Therefore, they are not to blame.

In the same way, no one can criticise parents for innocently teaching their children conditional worth. If parents have unconditional worth themselves, they will bring their children up to be free of the burden of conditional worth.

Learning unconditional worth

Carl Rogers concluded that to reach our highest potential, we need to be free of self-doubt and believe absolutely in our unconditional worth. To reach that state, we need to have been brought up in an environment of unconditional worth from childhood. However, creating an environment of unconditional worth is a skill that needs teaching, and typically cannot be achieved without parents also having been brought up with a sense of unconditional worth. This is no help to adults.

There are a few ways to create unconditional worth in adults. One such process[15] involves intensive work on the core belief of worth, including an experience of 'unconditional positive regard' to create an emotional memory from which unconditional worth is carefully built. It takes time – anywhere from six months to four years – to integrate these beliefs and experiences, depending on the client's situation and motivation.

This work is based on some immensely valuable principles[16] beneficial to people experiencing impostor syndrome without requiring the more intensive work. These principles include reframing of concepts that arise from conditional worth, and introducing the notion of unconditional worth. By understanding common behaviours and their underlying causes, coaches can benefit their clients in specific ways.

These principles are presented here to give your clients significant insight, and relieve stress and negative consequences.

Lessons from trauma therapy

War can have a lasting and highly disturbing effect on soldiers. Up to 37% develop Post-Traumatic Stress Disorder (PTSD)[17] when they return from fighting, depending on the severity and longevity of the conflict, and its support at home. Symptoms include constant anxiety and hyper-vigilance, typified by a veteran soldier diving under the table when they hear a car backfire in the street outside. It is an immediate reaction that generates instant panic.

PTSD is notoriously difficult to treat in psychotherapy and sufferers can remain in a heightened state of anxiety for years, dramatically affecting their physical and emotional health. Many different approaches to treating PTSD have been tried, with disappointingly low success rates. In order to find a common thread, a meta-study was done of the published literature on different PTSD treatments,[18] and a surprising theme emerged.

The best results were consistently achieved where the psychotherapist held an attitude of unconditional positive regard towards their patient, regardless of the treatment procedure. The patient developed a trust that their therapist would be accepting and not judge them, regardless of their behaviour, progress, success or failure. What the patients actually needed was unconditional acceptance, without any hint of disapproval or criticism. This is an amazingly beneficial attitude for any coach to hold towards their client, and we'll explore it more in later chapters.

Unconditional positive regard also turns out to be the key to helping clients with the anxiety and hypervigilance associated with impostor syndrome. Clients describe a sense of waiting for someone to walk up and announce that there's been a mistake – they were hired in error or their mistakes have been discovered, and they need to leave their job because they're not good enough to stay. This is feeling of not considering themselves good enough is a very real emotional trauma, induced from childhood. They believe that their worth is conditional.

It can be hard to see this lack of unconditional worth as having come out of a normal childhood. The traumas in PTSD are big and obvious, but it's easy to overlook the slight but frequent disapproval children pick up from parents and teachers.

Unconditional worth and identity

Every human life is a precious miracle and every person is worthwhile.

When a baby is born, it is lovable and worthy without needing to do anything at all, not even open its eyes. As we grow into adults, nothing changes; our value is not diminished. The only reason we don't believe that truth is because we've been taught the lie that we need to earn our right to life and love. We've learned that the opinions of others says something about our inherent worth.

By contrast, if we'd always felt valued and worthy, then we would never care about anyone criticising or judging us, because we would know that their opinions would not change our worth one bit. Any mistakes would be learning experiences; failure would simply inform us that our attempt didn't work. There would be no sense of shame or not being good enough, because we would know that we are good enough whether we succeed or not. We would be fearless in our pursuit of achieving our best, not because we need to prove ourselves, but because it would be fun.

Without the worry of what people think about us, we would naturally be open towards other people, sociable and friendly. We would recognise their inherent value and naturally care for and respect them. We would be consistently calm, warm and confident.

Summary

In this chapter, we saw how conditional worth is a lie we were taught to believe in childhood, and is shared by practically everyone we know. It keeps us stuck trying to earn a sense of worth in every new situation, which is precarious and exhausting. There's no-one to blame for people's lack of unconditional worth, as parents can't teach their children what they themselves don't know. But there are principles coaches can use to make significant strides towards helping people with this issue, including reframing and addressing the core belief.

Without unconditional worth, people unconsciously look for ways to feel better and more in control. Unfortunately, the behaviour patterns they develop can become addictive and keep them stuck in a cycle that reinforces the core belief of conditional worth. By understanding the behaviours, which we will take a closer look at in Chapter 6, we can help unlock the patterns, and in doing so release our client's maximum potential.

13. C. Rogers (1959). 'A Theory of Therapy, Personality, and Interpersonal Relationships, As Developed in the Client-centered Framework', in S. Koch (ed.), Psychology: A Study of a Science, Vol. 3: Formulations of the Person and the Social Context, New York: McGraw-Hill.

14. G. Baer, private communication, 2015.

15. T. Halliday, https://www.completesuccess.co.uk.

16. G. Baer (2003). Real Love, Rome, GA: Blue Ridge Press.

17. J. Gradus (2017).' Epidemiology of PTSD', https://www.mentalhealth.va.gov/coe/cih-visn2/Documents/Provider_Education_Handouts/Epidemiology_of_PTSD_Version_3.pdf

18. T. Weston, 'The Clinical Effectiveness of person-centred Psychotherapies: The Impact of the Therapeutic Relationship', PhD thesis, University of East Anglia, 2011.

CHAPTER 6

Conditional Worth-driven Behaviour

This chapter explores coping mechanisms for the ups and downs of a life based on conditional worth. There are many theories surrounding personality and motivation. After thirty years of exploring the subject, I'm going to present here the best framework I've found to describe people's inner workings.[19] It helps us as coaches understand our clients, and indeed ourselves.

Unconditional worth creates the calm, happy freedom to explore, challenge ourselves and succeed in every area of our lives. Our worth is a constant – it does not change, regardless of our actions, other people's opinions or circumstances.

When we believe our worth is conditional, however, we need to prove it continually. It is not something we can 'prove' once, because every day brings a risk of being found out to be worthless if we make a mistake. When we're on a roll and our results are good, then we feel great, because we've proved ourselves. However, when things go wrong, we feel worthless again. How we feel about ourselves then depends on our circumstances, which are often not within our control.

Emotional drugs

If people don't feel unconditionally worthy, they feel alone, empty and helpless – emotional pain. This is a terrible feeling, and they will do anything to avoid it. However, most people don't even recognise this emotional pain except in times of crisis or deep introspection. Much of the time, they feel like they're getting by. They view the ups and downs of daily life as normal, but it's a long way from the genuine peace and happiness of feeling unconditionally worthy.

The reason people can feel 'not so bad' is that they use a combination of emotional crutches, or 'emotional drugs'. These addictive emotional drugs offer short-term relief, but the 'dosage' people require is ever-increasing. They serve to numb or distract people from emotional pain rather than resolving it.

There are five emotional drugs:

- Approval
- Power
- Escapism
- Safety
- Drama

There is nothing inherently wrong with these behaviours. If we feel unconditionally worthy then they are simply pleasurable situations in everyday life. They become emotional drugs only when we use them addictively to numb or distract us from distress, or make us feel better temporarily.

Approval

Approval and disapproval are somebody else's assessments of us. They are simply opinions. But if we make someone's opinion mean that we are in some way not good enough, then we will always be fearing disapproval and needing approval. We will only believe someone else if they confirm our suspicions, or if we think their opinion is more valid than our own. Working hard to earn approval or to avoid disapproval is common among impostor syndrome sufferers.

Approval is fleeting and transient. We can work hard and be praised one day, make a mistake and be criticised the next. To earn approval consistently, we have to work very hard. People suffering from impostor syndrome are frequently extremely hard working. They are praised for having a good work ethic and producing results, so the message they have internalised is 'If I work hard and never make a mistake, then I will be valued'. It takes continual effort to stay in this zone of constant approval.

As many competent, successful people know, the higher their standards, the more people expect of them. Their hard work is assumed to be normal, and people around them expect them to produce their 'normal' results. So instead of being praised for their hard work, they merely satisfy those around them. If they are already working hard to get approval, then they have to work even harder. Overwork and exhaustion set in.

Approval as a hidden addiction shares the same features as a chemical addiction. Drug addicts become adapted to the level of drugs they take, which no longer produce the same high as before, so the addict needs to keep increasing the dose. Similarly, approval addicts get accustomed to a certain level of praise and expect it as their due. Their need for approval increases. But because they've made their high standards their norm, the approval they get actually decreases. In fact, they may only see the disapproval or disappointment when they make a mistake.

Most people have no motivation to stop another person approval seeking. After all, who is going to stop someone working extra hard to please them?

Case study: the golden girl

Elaine was the 'golden girl' in her family. Her parents held her up as a paragon of success. They would show her off to their friends as their talented, successful daughter, and berate her siblings for not being as good as her.

Elaine saw this as normal and played her role diligently. She knew that if she continued to perform well, she would attract praise and approval. She didn't even notice the effort she was putting in to winning approval.

At work, Elaine quickly rose up through the ranks and loved her job. As a senior executive, she continued to get lots of praise and play her golden girl role. Approval came not just from within the company, but also socially where her job title and obvious success drew more praise. She would never have noticed this pattern had she not left her job to start her own business.

She was excited by the entrepreneurial challenge, but found that she was at the bottom of the pack for the first time in her life. Her business was new, clients were few, and she didn't have an impressive track record to rely on as she had done in her corporate role. As a person addicted to approval, she was suddenly receiving none from her work. This became a great source of anxiety for Elaine, and the stress spilled over into her family life and personal relationships, with damaging effects that led to divorce. But still she couldn't see that the underlying problem was her addiction to approval.

Approval-seeking has certainly been my primary emotional drug, and the same is true for Daniel, our case study in Chapter 1. Even though it showed up in ways that looked very different in each case, the driver beneath it was the same for both of us.

Power

Power is the ability to get things done, get other people to do things, and to a large extent to have control over others. For someone who feels unconditionally worthy, power can be satisfying and fun; something to be enjoyed rather than depended upon. If someone does not feel unconditionally worthy, then power can be a temporary boost to avoid the helpless feeling that accompanies the distress of conditional worth. In that moment when they exert power, they feel strong and in control.

Many people find power addiction more distasteful than approval addiction. But approval seeking is manipulation, and is neither better nor worse than power addiction. We all adapt to our own ways of coping with emotional pain, and have a 'profile' of hidden addictions that worked best for us when we were growing up. They are simply a survival strategy we learned.

The saying 'power corrupts' describes an addiction to power. Just like chemical addictions, people get used to levels of power and require more and more to get the 'high' of feeling stronger. Rational judgments for the good of the team or company turn into decisions based upon gaining an illusory sense of power and strength.

It is common to see power addiction at top levels of management. This is precisely because managers have a certain level of power and become accustomed to it. They can then crave greater power, and it effectively becomes an addictive emotional drug.

A sense of power can be gained by people making their position visible to others through prestigious offices, cars, spouses and exclusive material things. People can derive a sense of power from the accumulation of things such as large property or stock portfolios.

Power can also be gained from making other people do things, and bullying is an extreme power-seeking behaviour. Using anger and attacking to get people to jump to attention or become afraid gives the bully a momentary sense of power and strength. But people do not develop close long-term relationships and communication with people that they bully. Bullies lack the human contact and support they need, and typically feel alone. When they reach for more power to stop feeling alone, they will create even more distance from others, which is how the addiction builds.

Life has a way of changing, and the loss of position can be devastating for a power addict. At best, power addiction is a temporary fix to emotional pain, but it is a precarious situation which leaves the addict vulnerable. Power addicts defend their position to protect the power they have.

Escapism

Escapism is a broader addiction. Typically, escapism addicts will jump from one distraction to another to make them emotionally numb. The other emotional drugs change the feeling rather than numb it.

Escapism is so common that most people don't regard it as anything other than the normal pleasures of life. Escapes are things that people commonly enjoy such as drinking, partying, entertainment and sport. When a person has a sense of their unconditional worth, these things are simply pleasurable. However, when they don't have that sense and feel empty, alone and not good enough, they reach for these pleasures as a way to distract themselves from the emotional pain. They become dependent on them to 'manage' their pain, fear losing them, which would mean they'd have to experience their pain, and so the pleasures become addictive.

Commonly used escapes include:

- Alcohol
- Drugs
- Gambling
- Shopping
- Social media
- Travel
- Food
- Sex
- Porn
- Extreme sports
- Video games
- Fitness
- Obsessive hobbies

I have used five of the above in a drug-like fashion myself. It's possible to turn any pastime into addictive escapism.

How can you can tell if a pleasure has become an addiction? If you are in any way upset at the idea of giving it up for a year – without substituting it with another escape – then it is. Of course, the exceptions are eating and shopping, which we all need to do. But if you notice you have a craving for certain foods or you're shopping when you're stressed and tend to over-spend, these activities are addictions.

Typically, people have more than one escapism addiction and will bounce between them. The classic example is people who give up smoking only to become addicted to sugary sweets. They have swapped nicotine for sugar, and the underlying need to 'medicate' their discomfort remains. You may argue that swapping from a physically destructive addiction to a more benign one is positive, which is true on a physical level. However, on an emotional level there is no difference. All escapism avoids emotional pain.

People recognise the destructive nature of some escapes, and completely disregard the significance of others. When they do recognise escapism in themselves, people can add an element of shame and self-recrimination to the addiction.

There is a disturbing sense of being out of control with escapist addictions. The cycle of binge-remorse is familiar to many – the remorse makes them feel worse emotionally, making them more likely to binge again to avoid the emotional discomfort.

Safety

An addiction to safety is not easy to spot in ourselves. We have to notice that we are not doing something and see a habitual pattern.

People addicted to safety will be less willing to put themselves forward for promotion and can be resistant to changes in their circumstances, role or situation. For people with impostor syndrome, this addiction will show up in specific areas and not across the board. Their safety comes from not making mistakes and risking the wrath, humiliation and rejection that they believe will follow.

For me, the avoidance was leading people, which I was very reluctant to take on early in my career. I am not by nature risk averse; in fact, I have a high risk profile in many areas. Avoidance is certainly not a broad brush to paint people with, and the same goes for all of the emotional drug addictions.

The safety addiction includes being unwilling to make a decision. This may be at home, work, financially or socially. The fear is the risk of making the wrong choice. Safety addicts conclude that making a wrong decision will mean they are worthless.

Controlling other people and their environment is another way that safety addicts behave. They can be overbearing and domineering; a safety addiction does not necessarily mean passivity. A person's strong need to control indicates they have an underlying sense of help-lessness. The belief is that if they can control everything around them, they won't have any surprises and therefore cannot be hurt.

Drama

The emotional addiction to drama is very common indeed. Drama can be apparent in the way people behave during an event, how they tell the story of that event later, or how they explain an anticipated experience in the future. It's like they're performing a play, exaggerating the events, their judgments, and their emotions.

The drama addiction has elements of seeking approval, power, escapism and safety. It may be used to:

- Entertain other people to earn approval
- Avoid feeling dull or boring

- Be right
- Manipulate
- Create crisis to avoid responsibility

The addictive part is the emotional roller-coaster people send themselves on when they make things a drama. Not only does the drama get a response from the people around them, but they also use it to feel more alive – or rather, to avoid the feeling of emptiness that may creep into their lives without it.

Entertaining other people to earn approval. Drama in its true sense is simply story-telling; engaging the attention of the audience. Professional entertainers use all methods of drama to tell a good story. However, people who are addicted to drama will make all their stories entertaining not for the pleasure of their audience, but for the approval they crave.

Drama addicts will bring in their emotion and be the hero or victim of their story, making others wrong or bad. A simple event can become a dramatic story. It is manipulation.

Avoiding feeling dull or boring. Some people have grown up with a horror of being considered boring. They feel obliged to be entertaining through dramatic stories and a dramatic lifestyle, as they feel their audience will disapprove of them otherwise. Unfortunately, that is true. If our friends are friends because we are their source of escapism, then they will disapprove of us if we don't deliver exciting entertainment. The drama addict is already in a trading game and will hate to get disapproval for being boring.

Being right. Some drama addicts have discovered that when they exaggerate a situation, their audience may sympathise with them. They then take that sympathy to mean that they were right and the other person in their story was wrong, making them the hero in a 'good versus bad' story. This is a method of feeling better by feeling superior, as being right gives people a temporary illusion of strength.

Manipulation. Making their discomfort or disapproval known by complaining loudly and aggressively is how some people persuade others to give them what they want, or avoid something they don't want. Manipulating others into guilt or embarrassment can be effective in controlling them.

Creating crisis to avoid responsibility. Maybe you know someone who seems to lurch from crisis to crisis. Each crisis is drama-filled and draws people in to rescue them from their situation. However, their crises are often due to their unwise decisions and their irresponsibility.

By creating a drama with a poor-me victim story inside, drama addicts attempt to manipulate people into allowing them to continue to be irresponsible. If they make their apparent emotional distress big enough, then their friends will rush to help them through the situation. But these addicts find their rescuers eventually tire of rescuing them.

Ultimately, drama creates a roller-coaster of emotional turmoil – high stress that is destructive physically as well as emotionally. By continually creating dramas, the drama addict doesn't get to experience peace, calm, gratitude and caring. Their lives are made miserable by the constant drama rather than being fulfilled or content.

Stress behaviours

When people don't have the emotional drugs of approval, power, escapism, safety and drama to numb their pain, they become fearful of the distress of conditional worth. They then turn to habitual patterns of stress behaviours. Typically this all takes place under the radar, as these are unconscious behaviour patterns. People only use these negative behaviours because they've learned that they work in the short term.

However, they never make anyone feel more connected or resolve the underlying distress. In fact, they make people feel more alone.

When we understand the driver behind them, then we can see that anyone exhibiting these behaviours is simply saying, 'I feel worthless'. Other people's stress behaviours are about them and not us, so we don't need to escalate a competition of 'who feels worse?' This changes everything in relationships.

The main stress behaviours are:

- Attacking
- Victimhood
- Lying
- Clinging
- Running

Attacking

Attacking is where people criticise or make negative comments about someone, including comments to make the other person feel guilty or ashamed. Essentially, attacking is wherever a person's words can be paraphrased as 'You're bad'. Attacking can be done with anger, which is most common, but also with superiority, judgement, sarcasm, or even as a 'joke'. People can attack others directly to their face or indirectly through gossip and snide comments.

Some people call attacking constructive criticism. However, if there is any hint of the attacker saying, 'You're not good enough', then it's not constructive, it's simply criticism.

Attacking can be non-verbal, and includes the attacker rolling their eyes, snorting or hmphing, pointed laughter, or any number of looks that say, 'You're an idiot'; 'I disapprove of you'; 'You're wrong', etc.

Attacking decreases a person's emotional pain momentarily by making them feel better than someone else. If the attacker makes out that someone else is wrong and at fault, then they believe they are right and blameless. Attacking is also used to manipulate someone to do something. It is a way of controlling people so that the attacker gets what they want. The belief here is that what they want will make them happy, and therefore take away their emotional pain.

But the problem with attacking is that it never makes anyone feel good in the long run. No one ever feels more emotionally connected to someone they have attacked. They may even feel guilty for their unkind actions, which increases their sense of being bad. Alternatively, they may hold on to the feeling that they're right and justified, denying they have done anything wrong even though they know they have acted unkindly.

Why is attacking unjustifiable? Because it is an expression of emotional pain, it is about the person doing the attacking and not about the recipient. When we attack someone, we are using them for our own brief pain relief.

Joining others in attacking someone can make people feel included and right – a brief rush of approval when they feel alone and bad. The proof of this is that when people are feeling completely comfortable, safe, relaxed, calm and happy, their natural human response to others is kindness and care. Humans are social beings, and our survival and strength come from co-operation. Our nature is to be kind and compassionate when we feel secure ourselves.

Victimhood

When we experience pain, we automatically hunt for the cause of the pain to make it stop. For physical pain, this works well – we can remove a stone from our shoe, for example. The self-preserving nature of our biology keeps us alive and healthy.

Emotional pain is less easy to spot if we don't know what to look for. Frequently, people look at others to try and find the source of their emotional pain, believing that the cause is immediate and right in front of them – 'If I'm hurting then I'm the victim here, and someone else is to blame'.

Victimhood is an insidious behaviour that places responsibility for our happiness and wellbeing in the hands of other people.

Lying

We are taught from a young age to 'protect' ourselves from criticism by lying. There is no scale for lies – a little white lie and a whopper are both the same. The motivation is to avoid disapproval and punishment or to gain approval, as we saw from Daniel's childhood experience in Chapter 2.

Clinging

When we reach for someone else to provide us with safety or approval, we are clinging. Like a small child clinging to their mother's skirt, we are saying, 'I'm helpless and you're obliged to help me'.

Clinging can be done in a whining way, such as 'Do you have to go out tonight?' It can also show up as excessive gratitude – a manipulation which effectively says 'Please do that again.'

Running

The classic responses to fear are fight, flight or freeze. Flight is running from a situation to avoid anticipated pain. The pain could be that a tiger is about to eat us, but few of us will ever meet a tiger. We use the same strategy as we would if we were faced with a hungry tiger to escape perceived emotional pain.

We may run from a situation by leaving our job, spouse, or an awkward social event. We run in relationships by withdrawing our energy, attention or affection from an interaction. The conversation ends because we have left it.

Summary

People are fundamentally caring when they feel unconditionally worthy. However, when they believe their worth is conditional, they feel emotional pain and a subconscious threat to their survival. To avoid feeling this pain, they adopt behaviours that act as emotional drugs to numb the pain or create fleeting moments of feeling OK. And when they don't get enough of their emotional drugs, they behave in ways that make other people give them the emotional drugs they need.

The root of all this negative behaviour is an unmet need to feel unconditionally worthy. This knowledge frees us from guilty feelings about the mistakes that we make. Of course, we still have a responsibility to make conscious positive choices as best we can, but failure to do so does not make us bad.

This principle enables clients with impostor syndrome to forgive themselves and others. It not only frees your clients from the guilt of their behaviours, it allows them to accept other people's choices calmly. After all, someone's negative behaviour is based on their own emotional pain.

In the next section, we will explore how we can use this principle to coach and help people through the emotional stress of impostor syndrome.

19. G. Baer (2003). Real Love, Rome, GA: Blue Ridge Press.

PART THREE

Coaching Impostor Syndrome

CHAPTER 7

Plan For Coaching

There is no one way to coach people. Coaching can be intermittent, informal and loose guidance, e.g. from a leader to their new team member, or it can be solution-based results-driven accountability and direction. Coaching can be slow, gentle support as clients navigate a difficult period in their lives. And coaching can be fast-paced, getting things done for clients stuck in a rut.

Whatever your coaching style and background, though, if you coach high-achievers, you will meet impostor syndrome sufferers. It will come up whether you're a life coach, business coach, team leader, mentor, counsellor or priest.

Your individual coaching style reflects your attitude, your philosophy and your experience. The client has their own personality and style, and will hear things you present in their own way. Therefore, this chapter is a broad brush on what approaches help with impostor syndrome sufferers. It is not teaching you how to do your job; my recommendations are based on what coaches need to help clients understand and overcome this particular issue.

A common coaching technique avoids any form of teaching or direction, and encourages clients to find and implement their own best solution to a problem. With impostor syndrome, however, there are solutions that your client is unlikely to have come across before. These solutions reframe the client's situation and provide immense relief from stress. Therefore, working with impostor sufferers includes an element of teaching. Coaches now need the self-awareness to strike the delicate balance of teaching without fixing.

An effective way to coach and teach simultaneously is to be completely transparent. This is especially important if you've been working with someone for a while and your coaching style has not included teaching before. While it may sound basic, a coaching plan is important for impostor sufferers. They actively look for disapproval or demands from you, whether they are conscious of it or not. A coaching plan makes it clear that their coaching sessions are not something they have to do well so that you will approve of them.

The process for an impostor syndrome coaching plan looks like:

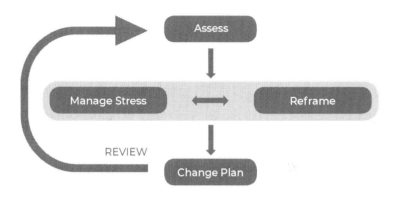

Steps 2 and 3 are done at the same simultaneously, as people need to manage stress while learning a different way of looking at the issue. For people under very high levels of stress, the stress management comes first, to move them away from dangerous situations. Sometimes this is done by referral to a GP for extreme stress. For this reason it is listed as step 2.

Step 1: assess

The starting point for all personal change is awareness. You need to be aware of the problem before you can address it.

Confusion is one of the hallmarks of impostor syndrome. People don't understand why they are feeling anxiety and stress. As capable, competent individuals, they are used to doing well in their career. They may also be confused about the level of stress that they are feeling – Not only 'Why do I feel bad?' but 'Why do I feel so bad?' Additionally, sufferers may not be aware that they are using stress-related or belief-driven behaviours. Instead, they may think that these behaviours are part of who they are as a person.

This was certainly the case for me around leadership. I saw my discomfort as meaning I was not a nice person, even though I believed I was. If I see that someone lacks awareness, I recommend they take the Clance Impostor Phenomenon Test.[20] This gives them an independently, verified measure of the issue that may resonate for them.

I've found that the problem is bigger than most people appreciate, and this is normal. It is important to explain to your clients that impostor syndrome is not weakness or failure. Step 1 is an information-gathering stage, and the facts must be seen before any changes can be made.

Mapping impostor syndrome

Explore the impostor behaviours outlined in Part One for clarity and create a plan for addressing each one. By tracking these behaviours, your clients can increase their understanding and reduce confusion. Simply tracking his impostor behaviours and understanding them would have helped Daniel in his law firm role.

Here are some suggested questions to help reveal impostor patterns. Rather than giving you a list to follow by rote, I have explained the purpose behind the questions so you can adapt them to your coaching style. Please do refine and improve on them.

Perfectionism

Are you a perfectionist?

Simple and direct questions work. A perfectionist usually gets a sense of pride or praise for doing things well. This means they're likely to recognise their perfectionism without shame. They don't appreciate how destructive it is to their wellbeing, so they don't think it's such a bad thing.

What activities are you most concerned about doing well?

People who think perfectionism means being perfect in everything will answer the previous question with a no. This question looks for impostor activities in which they may be a perfectionist.

How do you feel when you make a mistake in that activity?

The difference between high standards and perfectionism is the anxiety that an error causes. Perfectionists agonise over errors, have dramatic responses to their mistakes or go into overdrive to avoid making mistakes.

Deflection

Describe some compliments you have had for your work.

In calling your client's praise 'compliments', you're staying clear of whether it was true or not. Impostor sufferers believe that they don't deserve praise and may argue with you if you say otherwise.

Notice the sneaky use of the plural – you're suggesting that they get many compliments and are beginning to make that normal for them. This refocuses them to acknowledge successes.

Impostor sufferers may take a while to recall a compliment as their focus is on errors. Give them time to come up with something.

Hold back on pointing out any of their successes, even if you can list them. It's really important that they say what they have succeeded in to help them own their achievements. If you point out their successes at the start, you'll be yet another person they believe they're fooling and their impostor feelings will be made worse. You'll lose their trust and will no longer be in a position to help them.

What do you think about those compliments?

If your client deflects praise, the answer to this question will be a list of reasons why the compliments are undeserved. Explore their reasoning further to find out more about their viewpoint, but again don't try to convince them they're wrong. At this mapping stage, simply establish what their perspective is, and note to yourself where their perception is skewed towards a focus on mistakes.

Comparing

Tell me about your work colleagues.

This is an open invitation for the client to compare themselves with their colleagues. Impostor sufferers will feel isolated from their colleagues and see them as better in many ways. If they only tell you about their co-workers' successes, this can indicate a distorted perception.

Do you ever notice colleagues struggling at work?

Impostor sufferers focus on their own discomfort and may minimise or disregard difficulties their co-workers are having, revealing feelings of isolation. This question may surprise them, which is also a good clue. If it hasn't occurred to them that their colleagues have difficulties, then they are comparing how well their colleagues are doing versus how poorly they think they are doing.

Secrecy

Have you mentioned your stress to anyone?

The answer to this question will show whether your client has any other support, at home or at work. You will discover the degree to which they keep their fears a secret, which will give you a clear indication of the stress they are under. In Daniel's case, he told absolutely no-one, and even years later, he didn't mention his experience to his wife. Secrecy becomes a habit that can create a permanent sense of isolation.

You may find that you are your client's only source of support, in which case you can help them develop a support network going forwards.

Lying

Tell me about a mistake you made at work.

People lie and cover up mistakes in many ways, so this is a great question to gauge a client's level of anxiety around mistakes. You're not looking for the facts of the cover-up, that's irrelevant; you're looking for their tolerance of errors. Do they blame others? Do they ignore the question, change the subject or become defensive?

If someone has been referred to you by their manager or company, this question will not be useful. The client may fear their reply will be reported to their boss. You will need to judge the level of trust and rapport you have with your client.

Hiding

How easy is it to express your opinions in meetings?

You will discover whether your client keeps their opinions to themselves, and can then explore why. Their response will show whether they think their ideas are valuable. You may find out that they never volunteer opinions, first checking that everyone will agree with them so they won't be disapproved of. They may not be conscious of doing this, so it's worth asking if they offer opinions.

Have you declined promotions or not applied for them? Or hesitated to submit a business proposal?

Here you will see how they have held themselves back from further success.

When noticing these behaviours, clients need to be careful not to judge themselves or beat themselves up, which feeds the idea that they are not good enough.

Isolation adds greatly to impostor anxiety, and that includes the feeling that 'this is only me'. Simply informing your client that 70% of high-achievers experience impostor syndrome at some point in their lives can be a tremendous relief for them. Increasing awareness reduces anxiety, increases clarity, decreases confusion, and teaches people that it's more normal than they think.

Step 2: manage stress

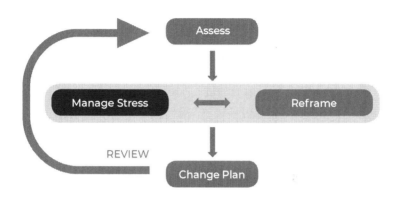

Direct treatment of the anxiety caused by impostor syndrome helps sufferers to manage stress through proactive choices. Many former sufferers I have interviewed have used personal stress-management techniques. These are positive coping mechanisms rather than escapist addictions. They include:

- Mindfulness
- Meditation
- Breathing techniques
- Tai chi and Qi Gong
- Biofeedback devices
- Gentle exercise

Mindfulness can be a powerful tool for relaxation, and *Mindfulness for Dummies* is a superb introduction to it.[21] For impostor syndrome clients, you'll need to be careful what they are being mindful of. Positive things to focus on include their breathing, and physical sensations such as their feet on the floor. However, mindfulness is not recommended for trauma victims and PTSD sufferers as paying more attention to their stressors may stimulate hypervigilance.

Meditation has been gaining more recognition as a useful tool. Its contribution to wellbeing, verified by neuroscience research, has made it more appealing. The only caveat is to make sure your client understands that it is not a goal-oriented practice aimed at removing all thoughts, which is a mistake over-achievers often make.

Similarly, breathing techniques are now taught in a stress-reduction context, and classes, books and guided breathing audios are easy to obtain.

Tai chi and Qi Gong are Chinese movement-based practices that include mindfulness, meditation and breathing techniques. As they involve slow, conscious movements, they calm down the client's whole physiology and are a tremendous help.

Biofeedback devices monitor heart-rate variability (HRV),[22] which is the variability in the length in between one heartbeat and the next. HRV is a clear indication of anxiety and frustration, and tracking HRV in real time provides direct feedback as to when other stress-reduction processes need to be used. It's very useful for people who like high-tech gadgets.

Gentle non-competitive exercise is also beneficial for stress release.

Encourage your client to experiment with any or all of these practices. Finding their favourite methods to manage anxiety and stress allows them to create a schedule for maintenance.

It's also a great idea to develop an 'emergency stress protocol' for when they become agitated. The protocol should be written on a small card, mobile phone note, etc. When people become stressed suddenly, their focus narrows onto the immediate situation in a normal stress response. This narrowed focus means people often forget their good ideas and intentions in the moment. Referring to a card in their wallet will remind them of what they need to do.

Step 3: reframe

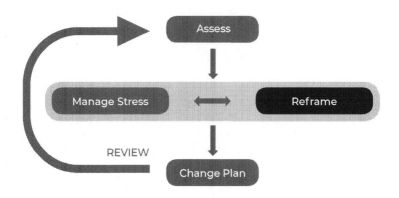

Now you can teach your client the underlying cause of impostor syndrome and explore unconditional worth.

Explaining to a client how they developed a sense of not being good enough in childhood is a delicate task as it can provoke strong reactions. It needs to be treated with care and compassion, but not fear. Typical reactions to this discussion in my experience include:

- Denial
- Anger
- Blaming parents
- Defending parents
- Shame
- Guilt

The table below shows the way clients may react to learning about conditional worth, the motivation for each reaction, questions you can ask to help them understand it, and the reframing you can teach. The overall answer is that they did grow up with conditional worth and their parents could not have taught them any differently. It's nobody's fault.

Client reaction	Motivation	Coach question	Reframing
Denial	The client has been praised for success. As long as they continue to perform perfectly then there is no problem.	What would happen if you did make a mistake?	You learned conditional worth via praise.
	They've seen others disapproved of, so the client worked at never making a mistake. Then there's no problem.	What would happen if others made a mistake?	You were taught conditional worth by witnessing others making mistakes.
Anger	The client recognises they 'should have' been raised with unconditional worth. They feel angry that their parents didn't give them that.	Did your parents know about or grow up with unconditional worth?	It was impossible for your parents to teach unconditional worth as they didn't know about it.

Blaming Parents	The client feels regret and a sense of 'poor me' about growing up with conditional worth, making it their parents' fault.	Did your parents know or grow up with unconditional worth?	It's not your parents' fault (as above). You can't change the past, but you can do something about it now. You're not helpless.
Defending parents	The client feels guilty and disloyal to be 'criticising' their parents.	Did your parents know or grow up with unconditional worth?	It's not your parents' fault. There's no criticism of your parents here.
Shame	The client believes it's their fault. If only they had been 'better' then they would have deserved to be brought up with unconditional worth.	Did your parents know or grow up with unconditional worth?	Your parents did not know how to bring you up with unconditional worth, so it's not their fault, and it's not your fault either.
Guilt	The client feels blamed or criticised for not being a perfect parent themselves.	Did you grow up with unconditional worth?	It is impossible for you to teach your children unconditional worth if you don't know about it yourself.

Reframing beliefs

Overcoming impostor syndrome requires the client to learn new principles and reframe certain beliefs. Many coaches encourage their clients to come up with a solution to a problem by themselves. However, conditional worth is an unquestioned core belief, usually unconscious, and very few people are able to identify the problem, let alone find a solution for themselves.

Indeed, society has no examples of unconditional worth, except in the most revered spiritual teachers through the ages. A 'holy life' seems unattainable or undesirable as it often entails withdrawing from the world and relationships. Unconditional worth is attainable, but people can't make a choice they have never seen, and the solution is not an obvious one.

The reframing principles include:

- I am unconditionally worthy
- Others suffer from conditional worth too
- Everyone always gets to make choices
- Expectations become a source of stress
- With choice comes responsibility
- Anger is destructive

- Accepting our mistakes makes us happier
- Mistakes are a necessary part of learning

These principles release the distorted thinking and free people to achieve more, feel comfortable and enjoy their success.

I am unconditionally worthy

The most impactful way to reframe beliefs is to question the client's implicit belief that their worth is based on what they do. When you bring this question to the fore, your client can usually come to the conclusion that they are worthy. If they struggle with this, I have found that discussing the worth of a new-born baby can help. What does a new-born baby need to do in order to be lovable and worthy? The answer is, of course, nothing.

Then you ask your client, 'And what's changed between the day you were born and today?' The empowering answer is 'nothing', but you may get a variety of answers that reveal their belief in their conditional worth.

The value of a £20 note remains the same whether it is brand new or old and crumpled. Equally, your client's worth remains the same. This point will need reinforcing. Most people have been taught throughout their childhood that they need to earn their worth.

Now your client understands that their behaviours and emotional addictions are symptoms of impostor syndrome, you can explore the habitual things they do when they believe that their worth is conditional. This releases their judgement, guilt and shame about themselves, which alleviates their confusion and helps them become more accepting. Their self-acceptance is paramount in reducing stress and anxiety. Behaviour patterns don't make them bad or unworthy; they are simply indications that they are believing in conditional worth, which they can change once they become aware of the fact.

Others suffer from conditional worth too. We think about other people in a similar way to which we think about ourselves. If we see that our unproductive behaviours and failings are a result of emotional pain, then we can see that this is true for other people, too. You model this attitude in your coaching through your acceptance of your client as they are, holding them to be worthy regardless of what they do or don't do.

Reframing the client's belief by showing them that another person's behaviour is a result of their own emotional pain, and nothing to do with the client themselves, is powerful. It takes the client out of victimhood and blaming instantly, and removes the pain of being criticised. They can then reflect upon feedback for the useful information it may contain, but the emotional aspect of feeling judged disappears.

A remarkable shift happens when we assume unwarranted criticism, blame and attacking is due to the critic's pain. When we don't feel that someone is making us bad, then our natural cooperative human nature emerges. We have compassion for them and want to help them if we can. This is different from trying to be 'stronger' than the other person and fighting to determine who is right; this understanding creates instant calm and relaxation in the face of judgment and criticism, and releases fear from the equation entirely.

Everyone always gets to make choices A source of stress that is so common, most people don't notice it, is the idea that there is a way in which we *should* behave. People argue from moral, spiritual and rational perspectives that some behaviours are acceptable and some are not.

A liberating way to reframe this is that everybody has the right to choose what they think, say and do. This is the same as completely accepting people and not judging them, but it goes a little deeper because people's choices affect us, too. If we think, *they should not do this to me*, we become afraid that accepting other people's choices will hurt us or we will lose out. We will be worried about being a doormat and not getting what we want in life.

The concept of a right to choose applies to us and our responses to other people. Just because someone moves to hit you – their choice – does not mean that you can't choose how you respond: fight back; move away; call the police etc. Their choices don't make them bad, and your choices don't make you bad.

If you're envisaging a world of complete anarchy, then relax. There's another part of the reframing of choice; people are always responsible for the consequences of their choice. We can choose to break the law by speeding, but the consequence can be a fine, our driving licence revoked, or spending some time in jail.

Expectations become a source of stress

When other people don't do what we expect them to do, it can be frustrating or disappointing. Maybe we have asked them to do something, or we think they should 'just know' to do something, or we expect that 'if they cared (about me)' then they would do…

Expecting people to do what we want is requiring them to consider us in their choices. However, if people are really free to choose what they say, think and do, then our expectation is a thinly-veiled demand that they give up their right to choose. People will still do what they choose to do, whatever their motivation may be. So having expectations only makes us frustrated, disappointed and unhappy.

Contracts are an exception, as both parties have agreed to the terms. Nevertheless, breaking a contract is always an option, and the penalties for that are consequences each individual is responsible for.

With choice comes responsibility

We are responsible for ourselves and our own happiness. When we are free to make any choice we like and prepared to accept the consequences of those choices, both the good and the bad. Then we are in a position to truly take responsibility for our lives.

If we ask someone else to make our choice for us, then we are abdicating our responsibility. So if things go wrong, blaming the person whose choice we now disapprove of does not help. We are not responsible for the happiness of others, nor are we obliged to make someone else happy. Their happiness is their responsibility.

This principle is not free rein to be unkind to others. We are happy when we feel worthy, are caring to others and are responsible for our own happiness. Unkindness not only affects the person we're being unkind towards, but it hurts us, too.

Anger is destructive

The principle of zero tolerance towards anger is a cornerstone of living a calm and successful life. Just like unkindness, anger is damaging to the person being angry. We not only feel disconnected from the people around us, but scientific studies have shown the destructive effect of anger on our physical bodies: damaging the cells, organs and cardio-vascular system.

Any time we are angry, we are thinking only of ourselves – how a situation may be bad or painful for us.

Accepting our mistakes makes us happier

Perfectionism, over-preparing and feeling like a fraud are the result of being intolerant of our own mistakes. Reframing our belief to see that mistakes don't make us bad frees us from that.

I often use the example of a baby learning to walk. When a baby falls down, it is not regarded as failure, but a normal and necessary part of learning to walk. Unfortunately, when an older child loses coordination of a body that is rapidly changing size and spills her drink on the dinner table, fewer adults accept that as normal. Their disapproval, even a sigh, teaches the child that the mistake has made her unacceptable.

Perfectionism, whether actively taught through punishment or implicitly taught through subtle disapproval, creates zero tolerance for mistakes.

The problem is not having high standards and working appropriately to achieve quality results; the problem is having impossibly high standards and working insanely hard to reach them. This leads to self-beating with judgments for the tiniest of imperfections.

The impostor mindset of anxiety, distraction and hyper-vigilance is the exact opposite of what our clients need for open, creative thinking. If they are intolerant of mistakes, it makes them less able to formulate effective solutions to normal business problems. They will be unwilling to make bold innovations for fear that they will be too much or simply wrong.

If someone bases their worth on their creativity – artistic or writing, for example – then impostor syndrome will make them unable to produce their best work. Unfortunately, this increases their sense of not being good enough and their emotional balance spirals downwards. Developing tolerance for and accepting mistakes is critical for their ability to be creative in the future.

Mistakes are a necessary part of learning

Here, we reframe the *necessity* of making mistakes, which addresses the impostor patterns of avoiding, lying, hiding and not taking risks. Their judgment that a mistake makes them bad creates an impossible emotional attachment to mistakes, convincing the impostor sufferer that mistakes are to be avoided or covered up.

Mistakes are part of the experimental process. We try something. If it doesn't work, we learn from that and try something else. The problem comes when people make their mistakes mean something about them.

People who are unafraid of making mistakes, who have mastered an emotional detachment from them, are truly free to create and achieve great things. A classic example is Thomas Edison, who worked on creating the light-bulb over and over again, trying different materials and designs. A thousand mistakes later, he succeeded.

Step 4: change

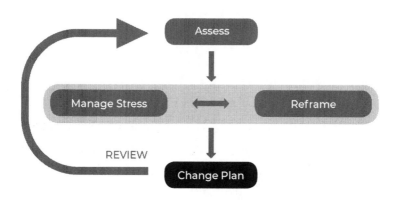

The route to mastery in any area is to refine one thing at a time. For example, a tennis player can spend an entire training session working on one aspect of their game. Neuroscience supports this concept in studies of focus and attention.[23] We do our very best work by concentrating on one thing at a time.

Your client will likely hate this idea. They're used to overworking, multitasking and resolving problems as quickly as possible. But changing impostor behaviours can be slow.

The more deeply a belief is woven into your client's emotional patterns and identity, the longer it can take to create lasting change. Explain that to your client early on. You can't bake a cake faster by turning up the oven heat – you end up with a burned top and uncooked middle if you do – and it's the same with impostor syndrome. It can take time to see deep habits of thoughts and behaviour clearly and make a choice to change them. Any time they get distracted, tired or stressed, they will naturally fall back into old patterns.

A coach's work is to help clients stay focused on one thing at a time, and encourage them to stick at it if it's a slow process and they find it frustrating. It's perfectly OK if it takes time.

Gradual exposure

Gradual exposure is an effective treatment used by therapists to help patients overcome phobias.[24] The patient is introduced to the thing that scares them in a slow, controlled and safe manner. For example, with arachnophobia the therapist may start off talking about spiders or showing their patient photos of spiders, making spiders a safe topic for discussion. It gives phobics a new experience of being safe around the thing that scares them.

If the patient's fear is too big and, for example, they get upset about the number of legs a spider has, then the therapist may start by talking about ants and centipedes. Gradually, they'll introduce talking about spiders, and as that becomes more normal, the therapist will bring in photos. They may build up to the patient viewing a small spider in a glass jar, and many arachnophobes eventually get to meet a live tarantula.

The point is that the fear is introduced at a pace the patient feels comfortable with, gradually building small, safe experiences. These experiences overwrite their belief in the fear. This is a great approach to use for impostor sufferers, who fear making mistakes and being judged.

We'll use perfectionism as an illustration, but any of the impostor behaviours can be resolved using gradual exposure. Reframing perfectionism starts with discussing the concepts, including:

- Perfection is an impossible standard
- Mistakes don't make you bad
- There is a point of diminishing returns where improvement adds no further value

When you and your client have achieved some level of agreement over the truth of these ideas, then you can move on to gradual exposure. The easiest starting point will be getting your client to make a deliberate small mistake, even though they will probably be horrified by the idea. In an internal report, for example, they will make one deliberate spelling error – not a mistake that will harm anyone or lead to business problems. Your client then needs to circulate/present the report as normal, and you task them with sitting back and observing reactions to the mistake.

If someone points out their deliberate mistake, they can reply, 'Oh yes, you're right. I'll correct that right away. Thank you for pointing it out.'

You may have to role-play this reply, all the while being gentle and understanding that this is the edge of your client's comfort zone. You are creating a new normal for them. The chances are high that they have never been taught how to respond to someone pointing out their mistakes without feeling shame, humiliation or defensive.

Gradual exposure can continue with one simple spelling mistake until your client feels comfortable with making a deliberate mistake.

The next step is to ask them to point out their deliberate mistake to someone: 'Oh look, I've made a spelling mistake there. I'll fix that now.' Once more, they sit back and observe the reaction they get, come back and discuss it with you, and again, this step needs to be taken slowly and gently. By this time, your client will probably be surprised and delighted at how well other people respond to them admitting to a mistake. They get a new experience that a mistake is not a catastrophe.

As action-takers, your high-achieving clients will often want to push themselves hard, learn this lesson, and get through this 'stupid' fear as quickly as possible. This is the impostor syndrome showing up again, because they are not accepting that it may take time to learn. They may also want to gain your approval for being a good student. If this happens, slow them down and do not let them race forward. Gradual exposure is exactly that: gradual. Rushing it will add to their stress and anxiety, and can have the opposite effect to increasing their comfort around mistakes.

A lovely story to share is how Persian rugs are made. Traditionally, Persian rugs have a deliberate mistake in the weaving. It is an acknowledgement that we are human, and striving for perfection will only lead to unhappiness and stress. Indeed, it is considered arrogance to try to be perfect, since perfection is the realm of the divine and not humans. A deliberate mistake is an exercise in humility and acceptance of the self.

Goals and intermediate steps for gradual exposure in the other impostor behaviours include:

Impostor behaviour	Gradual step	End goal
Deflecting praise	Accepting praise without excuses	Owning success
Comparing	Recognising colleague struggles	No comparing
Secrecy	Sharing with coach	Larger support network
Hiding	Speaking up in meetings	Sharing ideas or applying for promotion
Lying	Telling truth about mistakes	Comfortable with mistakes
Procrastinating	Well-paced preparation	Owning success
Avoiding	Arranging training and support	Doing impostor activity comfortably
Over-preparing	Reducing time spent on project	Balanced work time
Not enough	Reality of already enough	Not going for more

In each of these, start with the impostor behaviour that is causing the greatest problem or anxiety.

Other people's opinions

Impostor syndrome stress often includes feeling trapped. Your client has been taught that they should behave in a particular way and they're bad if they don't. What people think of them – how others judge them – becomes crucial. This is the belief that someone else's opinion defines or validates them.

Step 5: review

Monitoring progress and undertaking periodic reviews are key parts of coaching, and are important for impostor sufferers. Typically, they devalue their progress and focus on what's missing. Reviewing their success journal is a great way for them to maintain a balanced outlook.

Test your client's levels of stress from time to time, and discuss their impostor behaviours and their coping behaviours. Success is rarely linear, so tracking progress regularly and making adjustments as necessary will ensure your client stays engaged and motivated, and continues to make progress.

Summary

Each client is different and will have different behaviours to address, which means each coaching plan will be different and will evolve as they improve. Taking your client step by step through the process of assess–manage stress–reframe–change–review will give them a powerful, practical structure with which to address impostor syndrome. They can repeat this process as they become more comfortable and reduce or eliminate their impostor behaviours.

This is the process for constant and chronic impostor syndrome, and also for infrequent impostor syndrome. How to handle flare-ups caused by impostor triggers and how to guard against them will be discussed in Chapter 9.

The way in which you interact with your client has an impact on how well they will accept and trust you. The next chapter looks at how to coach impostor sufferers to enhance their results.

20. T. Halliday, https://www.completesuccess.co.uk

21. S. Alidina (2014). Mindfulness for Dummies, Chichester: John Wiley & Sons Ltd.

22. D. Childre, H. Martin, and D. Beech (1999).The Heartmath Solution, New York: HarperCollins. https://www.heartmath.com

23. D. Goleman (2013). Focus, London: Bloomsbury Publishing Plc.

24. American Psychological Association, 'What is Exposure Therapy?' http://www.apa.org/ptsd-guideline/patients-and-families/exposure-therapy.aspx

Best Practice For Coaching Impostor Syndrome Clients

A coach may be the only person that somebody talks to about their impostor syndrome. Consequently, your interactions with your client will have a significant impact on them overcoming it. Ideally, you will be a neutral presence guiding them with unconditional positive regard.

This chapter describes the coaching attitudes and behaviours that are unhelpful to impostor sufferers, and the behaviours that really work. Things to avoid include:

- Praise
- Perceived criticism
- Disapproval
- Demands

If you notice your coaching style does not help with impostor syndrome, then you have choices: you can be careful to avoid that behaviour in your coaching sessions, you can disqualify yourself from working with people with impostor syndrome, or you can seek training to expand your skills. Just as medical professionals are guided by the 'Do no harm' maxim, coaching professionals are wise to do the same.

Praise

Our society sees praise as a positive thing to give and receive. However, praise is a form of approval, and done poorly it says, 'I am judging your efforts and finding them to be good – to me'. It is about how the person giving the praise feels, not the person receiving it.

Praise may appear to work well in coaching, because you hold people accountable. If they try to please you by following through on their commitments, it can seem to you that they are doing well, making progress and getting results. However, impostor sufferers have grown up chasing praise or avoiding disapproval. It can be the number one motivator for the success they have achieved.

If you develop a dynamic within your coaching relationship where you are praising your client's actions, then you have taken on the role of the judging parent. Then they may hide mistakes and failures from you and only present positive results for you to approve of. Consequently, praise does nothing to help. By hiding failures, people perpetuate their impostor syndrome. They do not feel 'seen' by you, and so cannot resolve their fear of not being good enough. You become one more person in their life who doesn't understand them, which increases their isolation.

How do you give support without praise?

Whether your client has a great breakthrough or a serious setback, your demeanour should be the same: accepting them without making anything a drama. Pay close attention to your tone of voice and facial expressions, and remain calmly positive. Remember that you are supporting them, so when they're successful, you're happy for them, not because you believe that was the right thing for them to do. Rather than expressing your approval, turn the feeling back to your client for them to assess.

'Did you have fun with that?'

'What did you learn from that?'

'How does that achievement feel?'

These client-focused questions help them tune in to what they're feeling about the situation and stop looking for an external judge to approve or disapprove of them. They also help the client to reflect on their success and take ownership of their accomplishments, unravelling the impostor behaviour of discounting success.

Perceived criticism

Some coaches have an assertive 'no bullshit' style of coaching, which can give clients a refreshing clarity and new perspective. If your client is suffering from impostor syndrome, however, they will be hypervigilant and may hear your comments as criticism even where none is intended. They may then bring their habitual pattern of working hard to avoid criticism into their coaching relationship. If you make comments that can be misconstrued as criticism, you can increase their fear.

Once again, facial expressions and tone of voice are crucial to demonstrate calm acceptance. It can also be valuable to discuss this issue with your client to make sure they understand you are not criticising them. Their normal pattern is to assume criticism, so you may find you have to remind them you are not criticising them again and again. You will gradually break their old patterns of looking for criticism by repeatedly accepting them exactly as they are.

Disapproval

When coaching impostor sufferers, you need to be mindful of any disapproval you may be feeling. Someone who is hypervigilant will sniff out disapproval, however well you may think you have hidden it. If you find yourself getting frustrated with someone's progress or actions, even outside of your coaching session, then this is a sign you are emotionally involved in their achievement.

Of course, it is normal for coaches to get involved – you care about your client's progress. If you care about their progress for *them*, then you are less likely to get emotionally attached. However, if you're concerned that their lack of progress may reflect badly on you, your reputation or your record, then your disapproval stems from your thoughts about you and not them. Coaches need to be scrupulously honest regarding their coaching relationships and work to make them as clean and helpful as possible.

Bearing in mind our earlier discussions about perfectionism, we can only do our best and mistakes are inevitable, for both clients and coaches. If you find it impossible to separate your needs from your client's needs in your coaching relationship, then discuss it with your supervisor or disqualify yourself from working with that client. If you continue, then your disapproval can make their impostor symptoms and stresses worse.

Demands

There is a fine line between holding someone accountable for their progress and requiring them to progress. You can tell if you're making a demand if you feel disappointed or frustrated when they don't meet their goal.

If you are a dynamic coach who likes to work with pace-setter people, you and your clients will be used to getting fast results. However, impostor syndrome takes time to unwind as your client needs to create new habits, which take time to instil. If you are disappointed or frustrated with their lack of progress, you are communicating to them that they are not good enough. This feeds into their fear; any hint of a demand makes impostor syndrome worse.

If you do feel disappointment or frustration, then focus on accepting that your client is as far along as they can be for now, and that's OK. There's no rush.

Coach's unconditional positive regard

As we discussed in Chapter 5, the most significant results in PTSD recovery are achieved when the therapist holds an attitude of unconditional positive regard towards their patient. Although we as coaches are not dealing with extreme trauma, this finding still applies to us in my experience as the attitude holds tremendous power.

'Positive regard' is viewing your client as a valuable and worthwhile person. Unconditional positive regard is maintaining this view irrespective of what they do, say or think. This is essential to helping someone through impostor syndrome, because it is an issue that runs deep and touches on your client's identity and sense of self.

The range of attitudes that unconditional positive regard encompasses is significant:

- Accepting (not judging) actions
- No drama
- No disappointment
- No frustration
- Gentleness
- Patience
- Respecting choices
- No fear

Accepting actions

Humans do dumb things, guaranteed. Everybody makes mistakes at some point.

You and your client have agreed goals together, and they have committed to taking certain action. But by the next session, they may have done something else instead. Perhaps you planned one approach together, and then they completely messed up the timing or implementation. Essentially, they will have made mistakes and may not feel good about them.

If you join them in judging their mistakes, you are adding to the problem. Whatever they have done, no matter how significant the mistake, the destructive aspect is their own judgment that their mistake makes them bad, worthless and not good enough.

If you hold an accepting attitude, your client will be relieved and more able to accept their mistakes, too. You therefore model acceptance for them.

No drama

After making a mistake, your client may magnify their error and behave as if it is much more damaging than it actually is. They may get emotional, angry at themselves, blame themselves or others, panic, or feel overwhelmed. The mistake has become fuel for drama that distracts them from solving the problem. The drama will add to their sense of not being good enough, and make the error more significant and proof of their flaws in their eyes.

You can waste a lot of coaching time by joining in the drama, catastrophising, and listening to someone worrying over the impact of a mistake. It is more helpful to stay completely calm and downplay the scope of the error. Whatever has happened is not a disaster, even if it is a really big mistake.

Reframing the mistake helps to remind the client that it is simply an event. No amount of worry or drama can change it now; it is what it is. Your next step is to get them to accept the mistake and then resolve the issue the best way they can. There will be natural consequences of their mistake, and they will be accountable. However, this accountability can be reviewed calmly, without drama or judgment. This will help the client feel less isolated. They now have evidence that you will not blame them or regard them as bad or worthless for their mistake. It's just a mistake, and everyone makes them.

No disappointment

It's easy to get caught up in someone's development. They've defined goals they are passionate about, and you reflect back to them their dreams and plans. You are on board for their journey, supporting them and celebrating their success with them. It creates an emotional connection.

When they then fail to meet a target, it can be easy for you to feel disappointed. You may be disappointed for *them*, or you may be disappointed for *yourself*. Whatever the reason for your disappointment, you will unintentionally communicate it. Even people who have a great poker face reveal their thoughts through their gestures, facial expressions, tone of voice, or slight withdrawal of engagement.

If an impostor sufferer gets a confirming signal that you are disappointed in them, they will interpret it as the fact that they're not good enough for you. They are back to earning approval and will not be able to feel comfortable in that environment.

No frustration

We have a great position as coaches to observe some truly remarkable people for whom we will have respect and admiration. This is especially true when we're working with high-achievers. Their courage and determination are inspiring, and it is an absolute delight to work with them and help them achieve even more.

When we see someone's brilliance so easily, it can be frustrating to watch them sabotage themselves or their work, or make simple errors, or start doubting themselves. We know they are 'better' than that, and can become invested in their success and come to expect great things from them. There seems to be no reason why they should not achieve the next step.

If you find yourself in this frame of mind, you have unwittingly slipped into a role your client would have seen from parents or teachers. Because they are so capable, parents and teachers would have always expected them to be so and held them to high standards. Any frustration you have is similarly an indication of your expectations – because your client makes so few mistakes, you expect they won't ever make mistakes and get frustrated when they do, especially the dumb mistakes. This is buying into their perfectionism.

Any frustration or expectations will reinforce their impostor feelings and make the situation worse. Even when you try and hide such feelings, your client will be vigilantly looking out for them and will pick up on them.

Sometimes your frustration may be with yourself. You may blame yourself, your coaching skills or your approach for your client's lack of progress or mistakes. But even though you are not frustrated with your client, they won't know that. They will only pick up on your frustration and add it to their internal proof that *they* are unacceptable.

Gentleness

Many high-achievers have a dynamic personality, and are charming and confident. Their air of strength, which is genuine, can often give the impression they're invulnerable.

As you help your client through things they are struggling to do alone, you are a witness to where they are not currently strong and clear. Even so, they may still appear to be holding things together comfortably. This is a habit for them, and they may not be fully aware of how much they're hiding.

As they begin to address their impostor feelings, they touch into a painful area. Feeling less capable than usual can in itself be a scary place for them. It's therefore important for a coach to be gentle at this time. When you respect their pain and struggle by being gentle, you allow them the emotional space to become vulnerable. You will be seeing their flaws, the things they dislike or hate about themselves, and you will be accepting them in that place, which will help your client more than anything. This may be the first time that they have felt truly accepted, and it can be a tender and healing moment.

This will be true whatever kind of coach you are. Your awareness and sensitivity to impostor feelings can be a tremendous gift for any client.

Patience

High-achieving people are used to completing projects and tasks quickly, efficiently and to a high standard. They expect that once they understand something intellectually, they can then move through to a solution.

When they're working through their impostor syndrome, however, the process may be slower than they are used to. Your client will be changing habits and thought patterns of a lifetime, and real emotional change can take time. They often become frustrated with this; they may feel that they are somehow failing if they don't 'get it' quickly enough; it may even add to their feeling of not being good enough, making things worse.

Sometimes coaches get impatient with the process, too. Often we choose clients whom we have a connection with and who think along the same lines as us. A high-achiever often selects a high-achieving coach. This is a trap to watch out for, as you will communicate your impatience. The client will feel your impatience and get frustrated that they can't deliver results to you fast enough. Again, this will add to their discomfort.

Respecting choices

Clients may go directly against your suggestions, ignore your advice, and deviate from the plan they agreed to, but they'll have their reason for it. The reason may be fear, needing to be right, addictions or sheer contrariness, or they may just be testing you and watching you closely to see your reaction, much like children test boundaries by going against their parents' advice. It's not about what they do; they are trying to find out if they can trust you not to be demanding or controlling, and this behaviour is likely to be completely unconscious on their part.

The most helpful thing to do is accept that they have a right to choose. They have a right to make mistakes, fail and make stupid decisions. However, the consequences of their choices also fall to them. If you are an ocean of calm acceptance, then they will have an easier time accepting themselves and their failures as being OK rather than making them a bad or worthless person.

One of their choices may be not to work with you further, which could trigger an emotional response in you. If you calmly accept their right to choose things which affect you, you are demonstrating the highest care and what is best for them. This is the unconditional part of unconditional positive regard: respecting clients and their choices, whatever they choose.

No fear

Being fearless in the face of confusion, frustration, addictions, volatile behaviour and poor choices is an invaluable gift. You create a psychologically safe space without disapproval, criticism or disappointment in which your client can move through their uncomfortable feelings.

Here coaches need to turn the spotlight of unconditional worth on to themselves. Whatever a client does, *your* worth is not affected. Whatever mistakes you make and whatever results your clients get, you are still worthwhile. What you do does not define your value. When you free yourself from defining your value by your clients' results or approval of you, then you become a fearless coach. Not indifferent, but deeply caring. Now you are in a position to be of valuable service.

How to practise unconditional positive regard

As we have seen, there are many common attitudes and behaviours that will undermine a fully supportive environment. We have outlined the proactive features of unconditional positive regard:

- No expectations
- No judgments
- Allowing choice
- Being patient and gentle
- Being fearless and calm

Holding this state is a skill that must be developed; it's not simply a natural result of being a good listener. It is also an ideal to aim for, not perfection to be reached immediately.

The way to achieve unconditional positive regard is to hold the following beliefs:

- My client is doing the best they can
- Mistakes don't make people bad
- I'm here 100% for my client

Let's look at each one in detail.

My client is doing the best they can. Your client is doing the best they can with the resources they have. By resources, I mean their physical, emotional and mental capacity *in that moment.*

For example, just because they have done something in the past does not mean they can repeat it today. They may be overtired and not able to think so clearly. They may be stressed and distracted. They may feel overwhelmed and can't bring themselves to challenge a colleague as they have before. They may have lost interest in a project. They may have some hidden fears which have changed their view. Or they may simply make a mistake.

When we as coaches view our clients' actions and words as the best they can do based on all the resources available to them in that moment, then our emotional reaction changes. We instantly move to an attitude of compassion and concern. We accept what they have done without criticism, which is exactly what impostor sufferers need.

We need not explain our viewpoint to our client. Indeed, if we try, they may not understand or argue the point. This is due to their own high expectations, inability to accept their mistakes and need for perfection.

Mistakes don't make people bad. A great way to reframe mistakes is that people are fundamentally kind and compassionate when they are calm and not in emotional pain. Any negative, destructive behaviour is simply a person expressing, 'I'm in emotional pain'. This goes right across the spectrum of actions, from a cross word to a cruel and violent act. I am not condoning negative behaviour, as we always hold people responsible for the consequences of their actions, but we simultaneously *understand* that the cause is their emotional pain. This allows us to accept people's actions without making them bad. When we hold this viewpoint, we communicate it to the people around us and they feel more relaxed and accepted.

Impostor sufferers need your absolute acceptance without judgement, and you will possibly be the only person they have ever met who is able to give this to them. Do not underestimate the powerful effect of this attitude.

The other way to reframe mistakes, which I encourage you to share with your clients, is that mistakes are opportunities to learn. In fact, we can only learn from mistakes. Rather than feeling terrible for making a mistake, your client can look at what it has taught them. Where can they make changes to prevent that mistake happening again, catch it sooner or monitor for a recurrence?

This reframing only works when your client is not making themselves feel bad for the mistake. If they are stuck in an emotional 'I'm not good enough' loop, they will not be able to learn the lesson of a mistake.

I'm here 100% for my client. You can only hold unconditional positive regard when your client is the focus of your attention. Any time you drift into thinking about yourself – 'What's in it for me?', 'How will this affect me?' etc. – you are no longer present for your client. This is a learned skill because we automatically assess situations and how they impact us and our future. It is our inherent survival mode.

Meditation uses a technique of observing thoughts and letting them pass like clouds across a blue sky, without trying to stop or suppress them, and without worrying about them or focusing on them. Your coaching sessions could develop the same technique. Thoughts about yourself drift in to your mind: what this situation means for you; your judgements; how this might inconvenience you etc. See these thoughts and say to yourself, 'No, I'm here for my client now.' If you want to consider the thoughts and make further choices, you can do that later. If you keep bringing yourself back to your client's needs and happiness, you will be powerfully present and focused on them.

Coaches' blind spots

This book is designed for experienced coaches looking for an in-depth exploration of impostor syndrome. 'Blind spots' is not a section I should have to write, right?

Talking about blind spots can have the ring of harsh judgement to it, but criticism is not the intention. If you put aside any thought of criticism, then a blind spot is simply a description. It is a misstep that takes you out of unconditional positive regard and into being more concerned with yourself. You're then less available to help your client, and it may take effort to bring yourself back.

A truism in coaching is 'You don't know what you don't know', i.e. 'You can't see what you're blind to'. Please read on, and if none of this section is relevant to you, that's an indication that you've got this well covered. As someone who finds self-awareness fun, I enjoy anything that highlights common blind spots. I hope you do too.

Money. A coach has a constant turnover of clients working through their issues. Random cancellations, changes of plans and changes of circumstances are common. There is also a typical view that coaching is not a necessity but a nice-to-have. You and I may agree that this is when people need us most, but it doesn't help. The result is that there may be fallow periods when you don't have as much work as usual.

Regardless of how much we charge, we get used to an expected level of income. Fallow periods might make a coach more concerned about money than usual. This can create an attachment to retaining existing clients, and the unconditional nature of our coaching relationship will be eroded.

Results. Coaches can become as attached to results as anyone. Our clients come to us for help and state their goals. When they achieve their goals, it can look like it's because of us. It is so easy to feel like the hero – we've saved them and made their dreams come true. Especially if they give us effusive praise, we can start to believe that our worth as a coach depends on our clients' results.

In this situation, coaches can become subtly demanding. The demand can sound like disapproval when clients don't stick to their plans, or obvious approval when they succeed. Approval is 'I like how you make me feel', whereas being happy for clients is being pleased that they are pleased with their results. While this is a subtle point, the approval-disapproval axis is at the heart of impostor syndrome and conditional worth. It takes conscious attention to watch out for this trend.

Reputation. Similar to deriving a sense of worth from results, we can attach our worth to our reputation. Then we may worry that poor results will make us look bad and damage our reputation. This can be linked with money concerns, too, when we fear that a dissatisfied customer will hurt our chances of getting new work.

At this point, we now fear our clients' disapproval, which will change the way we interact with them. When we fear our clients, we focus on ourselves and not them. We are not as available to accept them for who they are.

Agenda. One of the trickiest things to do in coaching is to keep our mouths shut when we have an opinion about our clients' decisions. If we track ourselves carefully, we may see that we have developed a need to be right in our life. Being right is not a problem, but the need to be right is. From here, it is all too easy to try and influence our clients. Our body language and tone of voice will reveal our opinion, as will not-so-subtle hints and nudges in the 'right' direction. It takes awareness of our motivations to allow someone to make a decision with which we disagree.

Supervision. When I first trained as a holistic therapist, the college emphasised the importance of continuing su-pervision. A supervisor would help me navigate tricky situations with clients, and make sure that my own concerns in life were not spilling over into my coaching sessions. They would help me be there for my client and not let subconscious behaviours blur the boundaries with my clients.

After I had been working as a therapist for over ten years, I had encountered all the difficulties and could navigate unusual situations by myself. I had fewer supervision sessions until I stopped them entirely, as I didn't seem to 'need' them. And that was my big mistake.

When I started to go downhill emotionally, as I mentioned in the introduction, I still didn't get supervision because my client sessions were the only thing that *was* working at that time. In those sessions I could put everything aside to be with my clients and it was a brief respite from my concerns.

What I didn't see was that I needed support and that even though my problems weren't affecting my clients, if left unchecked, eventually they would. In my case this played out as me needing to take a six-month break from working with people so that I could get myself back in balance. We frequently see the consequences for clients when their coaches, therapists, gurus and teachers have started to have problems, have become enmeshed in their clients' lives, lost perspective and made rash choices. In any role as a trusted guide, on-going supervision is essential no matter how many decades we've been practising.

My own college teacher was an exemplary role model in this regard. She was at the top in her field, ran a prestigious and highly-respected training programme and had been doing so for over 30 years. And she still had regular supervision. Not from a 'superior'– there were none of those – but someone capable of seeing her clearly and keeping her on track personally and ethically.

From my own experience, the mistakes of people who failed to have supervisors, and the good example of my college teacher, I have learned that regular supervision is essential throughout your working life as a coach.

The solution for blind spots is to pay attention to your motives, and be aware of your own habits of thought and beliefs. It's likely you've been examining yourself as you've been reading this book, which is great.

Summary

In this chapter we covered the guidelines and best practices for coaching impostor syndrome clients, as well as what not to do and blind spots to watch out for.

If you develop the skill of unconditional positive regard, you will find it exhilarating, not draining. You will develop a level of detachment from your clients' choices without losing care for their wellbeing. Your emotions will not be triggered to become involved in your clients' dramas, and you can coach someone in deep pain while maintaining calmness and care.

Combining what we've learned in Chapters 7 and 8, we can now work on strategies for coaching clients through trigger situations and helping them create a healthy work environment.

CHAPTER 9

Workplace Strategies

In this chapter, we will look at how to deal with the impostor syndrome triggers of change and challenge, and a toxic workplace. The strategies covered in this chapter can be used while your client is in the middle of a stressful situation, or pre-emptively before the triggers become a problem. We'll also explore ensuring any new environment is not toxic for sufferers of impostor syndrome.

Managing the change/challenge trigger

We saw in Chapter 1 how Daniel's impostor feelings were triggered by a new role and the challenge of working with a top-notch team. So if such change triggers impostor syndrome, is the solution for the sufferer to avoid all new challenges?

Not at all.

People derive a huge sense of achievement and satisfaction from success in an arena where they have not tested themselves before. This is what makes challenges exciting and fun. You can prepare your client to meet challenges head on and enjoy the success they bring, but they will need to do certain things differently if they are to thrive in challenging situations rather sink under the stress of impostor syndrome.

There are five key areas to develop to make any challenge exciting:

- Awareness
- Skills shortage
- Asking for help
- Saying no
- Celebrating success

With these, your client can plan to manage the challenge trigger proactively.

Awareness

When you have identified your client's impostor activities, then it's easy to see where a new role or project may exacerbate them. Map out the activities in this new situation and match them up with your client's impostor activities. This clarifies what may trip them up, and you can both plan how to handle it.

Skills shortage

Some impostor sufferers expect themselves to be an expert before they have had enough training or experience. They are used to learning new skills quickly and easily, and assume this will always be the case. If you challenge this unconscious assumption, you may get a sheepish smile and acknowledgement their expectations are unrealistic.

For each skill required in the new project or role, ask your client to rate how competent they need to be and how competent they are. Where you find a skills gap, ensure they arrange appropriate training, and hold them accountable for asking for it.

They may be reluctant to request training, feeling that the need makes them look incompetent – i.e. a fraud. They may feel ashamed or embarrassed. In the strictest sense, inexperience *is* incompetence. However, it is fixable through training, and not an indication that your client is a fraud.

Asking for help

Often impostor sufferers believe that they need to do everything themselves. They believe that it is cheating or not really their success if they get help, or consider that asking for help is a sign of failure or weakness. Some people even have a sense of pride in never asking for help. This may sound like a classic men's issue, but it affects successful women equally.

Business is about teamwork – working together to get results. It's not individual heroes doing everything by themselves. You can help your client to get over this tremendous handicap by reframing the meaning of help. Sports teams can be a nice reference here – a team can't win a football match with just one person, no matter how good they are.

I've found it helps to point out gently that your client has already asked for help by engaging you as their coach. They clearly understand that sometimes assistance is necessary, but may need the support of a gradual exposure process described in Chapter 7 to ask for the help they need in a work environment.

Saying no

Some impostor sufferers take on too much. The idea of

saying no seems like an admission of failure. In a changed or new role, they will be tempted to keep saying yes and working manically to keep up, which quickly leads to burnout.

In a new role, your client's impostor feelings may create a need to prove themselves to be good enough. Even someone who usually turns down inappropriate projects may find themselves saying yes to prove they deserve their new role.

You may spot that they're overwhelmed before your client does. Indeed, they may deny or ignore that they have too much on their plate. It's helpful to check in with them about how well they are coping and actively look for areas of stress.

If someone is working at or beyond capacity when they first come to you, you can provide an objective view and help them see their inability to say no as a problem. This is disaster prevention. You can help them recover balance by encouraging them to tell their boss the truth about having too much on their plate. A useful way to reframe this is to let them know that everyone will find out they're overwhelmed one way or another, either when your client tells them, or when your client or the whole project collapses. It's far better for them to tell the truth and work to make sure the project has every chance of success.

If they are reluctant to reveal that they are over-stretched to their boss, they can develop the skill through gradual exposure to saying no, ideally starting with small, insignificant things, perhaps outside of work.

Celebrating success

When a high-achiever celebrates their successes and accomplishments, they have a balanced outlook. They will be more able to enjoy challenges in the future, rather than being driven by fear of failure. Focusing their attention on their successes will have a powerful effect. However, it is important that they are the one to identify the results that are satisfactory (successful), because then they take ownership. If you point their successes out, an impostor sufferer will secretly discount them.

A success journal is a useful way for your client to track their milestones, and it counters their tendency to focus on failures. Review their success journal on a regular basis so that they can keep their achievements in mind.

Mastering these five points will give your client the ability to grow and develop in their career. They will be able to meet new challenges with relish and enthusiasm, and enjoy the success they already have. It's a huge gift for them, and a spectacular result from their work with you.

Managing the toxic workplace trigger

Generally, successful people are resilient to disapproval, but a toxic workplace can trigger impostor syndrome. A toxic workplace can be a result of the company culture or just one person being negative, particularly if they are the boss.

A toxic environment has a pattern of negative comments, anger, criticism and intimidation. Bullying and its destructive effects are well understood. However, the negativity does not have to be as blatant as bullying to trigger impostor syndrome. It can also be triggered by changes in your client's boss's behaviour, causing your client to feel like they're suddenly out of favour.

If their boss's behaviour becomes erratic, impostor sufferers will often think that they are at fault, but volatile behaviour is a common reaction to stress. A boss who is critical, frustrated, angry and intolerant could simply be going through a stressful time, possibly even suffering from impostor syndrome themselves. This is how impostor syndrome can spread in a team.

A stressful home environment may also trigger impostor syndrome at work. High levels of criticism can cause the sufferer to become hypervigilant for disapproval, so even though the source of their stress is their home life, the stress will show up in their impostor activities at work. For this reason, it's always worth exploring a client's whole life situation, even if their complaint is about work.

Areas to address in a toxic workplace include:

- Awareness
- Addressing negativity
- Reframing
- Leaving

Awareness

A toxic workplace must be identified as a source of stress. Your client may not recognise this as a problem at first, so you can explore the possibility that their increased anxiety may be due to changes that have created a more critical working environment.

Many impostor sufferers believe that stress is normal. They have a 'suck it up' approach and try to push through and ignore their discomfort, or turn to addictive escapist behaviours. That is an unsustainable approach and the cost is high. Here, you can challenge their assumption that high levels of stress are normal or acceptable.

Some impostor sufferers fall back into an old habit of thinking that the situation is stressful because they are not good enough. This stems from behaviour learned in childhood. Children often assume that an adult's words and behaviours are correct, so if an adult criticises them, it must be their (the child's) fault.

Assessing the factual changes in the behaviour of people around your client or new behaviours in their environment is key. You can then help them see a balanced picture, as their impostor mentality skews their perception.

Addressing negativity

In realising that their stress is due to a toxic workplace, not their personal flaws, your client moves from helpless to empowered. They realise they can choose to make changes. They may choose to change their negative environment and come up with several ideas for doing so, but their scope for addressing the issue depends on the company culture.

Standard non-violent communication[25] approaches work well here. A private conversation with the person being negative may be all the client needs. If your client states clearly that this behaviour is unacceptable, and they will take action if it happens again, e.g. leave the room or make a formal complaint, it can prevent it happening again. If the formal discussion with the negative person doesn't work, your client can then escalate the complaint to a boss or the human resources department. Your client may even be able to lead a change in workplace culture and team behaviour.

Just seeing their choices helps your client feel positive, in control and not trapped. The sense of feeling trapped in a situation is a huge contributor to stress.

Reframing

Your client will benefit from reframing the negativity and their response to it. This requires you to work through their 'not good enough' belief.

A useful concept to share with your client is that anger and criticism are expressions of the emotional pain and stress of the person delivering them. People use anger defensively to get others to back off and protect themselves from further pain, or to get their emotional drug of power, as mentioned in Part 2. If your client can see that a person's anger is not about them, they can greatly reduce their own anxiety.

Imagine you are at a spa. You have had some wonderful

treatments and are relaxing in the warm sunshine by the pool, calm and comfortable. Would you be feeling angry here? I doubt it. Our natural state as humans is to be calm and co-operative.

When they can step back and see their boss and colleagues as being in pain themselves, your client's fear that they are being accused of being bad disappears. Then they are able to assess the content of the criticism calmly. Is it valid feedback? Is it relevant? Is there something useful to learn from it? This approach can make a previously intolerable situation manageable.

Leaving

It may be appropriate for your client to leave a workplace if the toxic people around them show no signs of being able to change. This is a difficult decision to make, but the long-term effects of staying are potentially too damaging.

Choosing to leave rather than leaving when the stress has become too intense are very different scenarios. Pro-actively leaving, your client takes control of their working environment. They demonstrate that they value themselves and are responsible for their overall wellbeing. It's an empowering choice.

Due to their high expectations of themselves, your client may see leaving a workplace as a personal failure. They may feel like they aren't strong enough (read 'good enough') to handle a difficult situation. If they do 'tough out' a difficult situation, they may feel temporarily stronger, but that attitude often leads to addictions or burnout. Here it's important for your client to make the distinction between taking responsibility for their own wellbeing and toughing it out.

Career change strategies

Your client will now understand:

- The impostor activities that are 'at risk' for them
- The trigger of change
- The trigger of a toxic workplace
- Intensifiers that apply to them

Once your client understands the triggers for their impostor syndrome, then they can make pre-emptive choices to minimise its impact. You can now help them choose the career path that offers much more happiness. They may look to change their role, company or industry. They could move from employee to entrepreneur or vice versa. Whatever their choice, they can make it from a place of understanding, being proactively responsible for their wellbeing.

If your client has a new role to consider, help them assess the situation for its potential to be a healthy environment for them. The following factors are useful to examine:

- Team dynamics
- Learning focus
- Exact role requirements
- Training available
- Mentoring support available
- Intensifiers

If the role is within the company your client already works for, it can be easy to ask their colleagues about the team. If the role is with another company, they need to pay attention to these issues and gather as much information as possible.

Team dynamics

The tone of a company is determined by the emotional intelligence of its leaders and teams. Key measures of emotional intelligence include self-awareness, self-management and the ability to work in a team.

At interviews, people tend to be on their best behaviour. If your client gets the opportunity, then they should make a point of observing interactions between team members. If they get the impression they're in a school playground with a bunch of five-year-olds, this is a warning sign. Immature behaviour such as sniping, casual insults, blaming and drama show how this team operates on a daily basis.

Learning focus

'What happens when someone makes a mistake?' This is a great question for your client to ask, then carefully watch the answer. They need to be looking out for blaming, shaming and anger. If a calmer attitude prevails, they may be on to a winner. If the management team in a company fixes the problem quickly and puts procedures in place to stop it happening again, this forms the basis of a proactive teaching and learning environment.

Exact role requirements

Junior roles tend to have clear, well-defined duties. By contrast, senior roles have a broader scope with an assumption that senior staff will do whatever needs to be done.

It's useful for your client to take a closer look at the exact requirements for a position, in particular identifying any unfamiliar elements to the role. If they discuss the new tasks with you, you can help them spot potential problems. Here you'll be looking for signs of their impostor activity. If they have been unconsciously avoiding a task, they might not recognise that it's an issue.

Ideally, any new role should come with training, coaching or mentoring to develop their skill and provide support while your client becomes competent.

Training available

Your client will need to ask for training, and you may need to assist them in this. Asking for help is often difficult for people suffering from impostor syndrome as they believe it makes them look weak and incompetent. Help them reframe their need for training as a deliberate choice for excellence. In order to be successful in their new project or role, they'll need to be properly trained and not spend time trying to figure things out by trial and error.

When they ask for training, your client is taking responsibility for their emotional wellbeing, valuing themselves, their time and energy. It is additional feedback to themselves that they are worth taking care of, which helps diminish feelings of not being good enough.

Mentoring support available

In addition to training courses, your client will ideally have access to mentoring. This one-to-one interaction develops excellence at all levels within a company. When they are assessing a new role or company, get your client to check the availability of mentoring from an experienced person, even if your client is at CEO level.

Intensifiers

Your client should look out for potential intensifiers of impostor syndrome as well as known ones. For Daniel, when he moved to the London law firm, he became conscious of his strong northern accent, which added to his sense of not belonging there. Before the move, he had never given his accent a second thought.

Even if your client discovers stress intensifiers in their new position, the fact they are aware of their thinking and have you to help them work through it means that the destructive effects of intensifiers will be much reduced, maybe even eliminated.

Throughout their career change planning, your client will be looking for indications that they will thrive in a new role. This puts them in an empowered mindset that they are doing the interviewing, checking to see that the setup is suitable for *them*. It's another way in which they are valuing themselves.

This is very different from feeling like they are being judged and assessed. Valuing themselves is a great way for your clients to combat the impostor feelings of not being good enough.

Summary

In this chapter, we looked at how triggers and intensifiers of impostor syndrome can be addressed proactively once your client is aware of their impact. Coaching them through planning in advance and managing an ongoing situation, you empower them to resolve impostor syndrome. Your perspective rebalances your client's distorted views of success and allows them to develop a calm, productive attitude to foster their maximum productivity.

25. M. Rosenberg (2015). Nonviolent Communication: A Language of Life, Encinitas, CA: PuddleDancer Press.

Conclusion

Congratulations!

You now understand impostor syndrome in depth.

Some advice suggests that sufferers should 'sort impostor syndrome out for themselves', but people cannot do this alone. As a coach, you are in a uniquely privileged position to be able to support and help people overcome impostor syndrome, which affects 70% of your high-achieving clients at some point in their lives. You now have the knowledge and tools to make a difference and get great results in your coaching.

Impostor syndrome is a huge stress leading to anxiety, isolation, burnout, stress-related illness, or simply giving up. It's not a lack of confidence or poor self-esteem. We've explored what doesn't work for sufferers of impostor syndrome and what can make things worse. Knowing the most effective way to help is vital.

The book has cut through the noise and provided a masterclass in spotting and understanding impostor syndrome, helping the sufferer not just to cope, but to overcome it. You now have a clear path to helping your clients get the results they really want – to feel good enough and enjoy their success.

As impostor syndrome is a phenomenon that typically includes secrecy, coaches need a detailed knowledge of how it manifests in high-achievers. You may need to play the detective with clients who are unaware of it or in denial.

Impostor stress comes and goes for most people, and there are two identifiable situations that trigger an 'episode': change/challenge and a toxic workplace. Knowing when your client is susceptible to these triggers means that you can address impostor syndrome early and minimise its impact, creating resilience strategies for when it does occur.

The gold in helping your clients overcome impostor syndrome comes from a thorough understanding of the underlying cause: conditional worth. People with impostor syndrome are usually confused, asking themselves why they are feeling stressed when logic says they have nothing to be concerned about. This confusion adds a sense of frustration, helplessness, and sometimes shame to their existing stress.

Your clients can reach for the greatest achievements they are capable of when they're not shackled by impostor syndrome. Developing a sense of unconditional worth frees them from the fear of other people's opinions and their own self-doubt, and is the secret to a happy and satisfying career. I truly hope that the knowledge you've gained from reading this book will enable you to help your clients reach their maximum human potential.

Acknowledgements

I'd like to thank the many sufferers of impostor syndrome that I interviewed in my research, who I won't be naming for reasons of confidentiality. Your willingness to share your experience of this painful situation means that many other people will benefit and hopefully suffer less as a result. Your open generosity will help many.

Massive thanks to my amazing test readers, who have shaped the book: Curtis Hurren, Ben Green, Andrew Priestley and Susan Payton. Thanks also to structural editor Dale Darley for a brilliant job of direction.

To the Rethink Press editorial team; Lucy McCarraher, Verity Ridgman, Alison Jack, Jodie Holloway and Joe Gregory, I love the way you've taken my ideas and polished them to give more clarity and understanding.

Thanks to Moe Nawaz for the original suggestion to write a specialist guide for coaches and mentors. You gave me a way to reach more people than I could ever have done alone. Thanks also to Daniel Priestley and Dent for encouraging me to write the book in the first place, and for your unrelenting support in putting it together.

Huge thanks to my accountability buddy Alex Seery – you have no idea how much you helped me to focus and to finish it.

Finally to all my amazing teachers over the years: I'm forever grateful.

The Author

Tara Halliday has been a holistic therapist and transformational coach since 2000 and has a lifelong fascination with human psychology, neuroscience and personal growth. She also has a PhD in Engineering – ironically due to her own impostor syndrome.

Tara's fear of being found out to be a failure and a fraud surfaced a few times in her life, and led to a disturbing overwhelm. She then discovered the value of unconditional worth, which changed everything. Even though her life circumstances continued to throw challenges at her, as life always does, she met them with calm composure instead of anxiety. Once, an experienced advisor even said to her, 'I've never seen anyone so calm in this situation. You either have a brilliant poker face or are genuinely happy.'

Tara has a terrible poker face.

Describing a problem and patching up the symptoms are not enough for Tara. She needs to understand what causes the problem in the first place. The experience of healing her own personal issues spans more than thirty years, and of working with others nearly twenty years, and it has led to her finding the underlying causes of impostor syndrome, and ways to resolve it.

She brings this work to the attention of executive and life coaches and mentors across the world in *Unmasking*.

You can find more about Tara at:

www.completesuccess.co.uk
www.linkedin.com/in/tara-halliday-phd/
www.facebook.com/complete.success.ltd/
www.twitter.com/tarahalliday1

Made in the USA
San Bernardino, CA
25 July 2018